AF600167

SPONSORS AT BAPTISM

according to

THE CODE OF CANON LAW

A DISSERTATION

Submitted to the Faculty of Canon Law of the Catholic University of America in partial fulfilment of the requirements for the Degree of Doctor of Canon Law

By the

REV. RICHARD JOSEPH KEARNEY, S.T.B., J.C.L.

Of the Archdiocese of Philadelphia

WASHINGTON, D. C.

1925

173,327

Nihil Obstat:

†THOMAS J. SHAHAN, S. T. D.,

Censor Deputatus.

Washingtonii, D. C., die XVI Maii, 1925.

Imprimatur:

†MICHAEL J. CURLEY,

Archiepiscopus Baltimorensis.

Baltimorae, die XVI Maii, 1925.

CONTENTS

FOREWORD

The study of the canonical legislation regarding sponsors at the sacrament of Baptism has both a practical and an historical value.

The administration of Baptism is not an infrequent occurrence. A knowledge, then, of the necessity of having a sponsor; the qualifications postulated by the law for one to validly or licitly function in this capacity, and the subsequent relations of the godparents and their spiritual children, are of no little importance. The Code introduces a change from the former discipline in the origin and extent of spiritual relationship as a matrimonial impediment. Not a few disputed questions of the past regarding this spiritual relationship find a solution in the disposition of the present law.

It is true that many of the Code's enactments concerning the ceremonial office of sponsor, though revised in some details, are substantially a succinct presentation of legislation centuries old. Wherefore a somewhat detailed historical treatment of the subject has been given in these pages.

It is the purpose of the present treatise to discuss the origin of sponsors at Baptism; to trace the development of ecclesiastical law regarding their number and qualifications, and to indicate the application of the Code's legislation concerning them.

CHAPTER I

The Liturgical Necessity of Sponsors

In setting forth the legislation governing the present discipline of the Church, it is not the purpose of the Code of canon law to deal with history, still, at times, there is a hint or suggestion proposed by the law-giver to indicate that the legislation being set forth is endowed with an historical background.[1]

The historical aspect of Church law is most attractive, for there is hardly a division of canonical legislation that has not a history both enlightening and interesting. Almost every department of law operative at present represents a crystallization and systematization of the legal forms of the past. The old adage that the present can be better understood in the light of events that have gone before is particularly true of the Church's legislation, for the history of the Church's law sounds the very depth of human nature, and reflects the sorrows, the humiliations, the joys and the triumphs of that glorious Church through the centuries. In that law we hear the voice of the Church, like the voice of a mother, echoing down the years, commanding, threatening, directing and encouraging her bishops, priests and faithful children.

Although the Code of canon law has introduced some changes from the former ecclesiastical discipline, the Code brings with it little that is new. The present laws of the Church, as embodied in the list of canons, are but the grand edifice erected on the legislation of centuries, which legislation has been revised and extended to meet the needs of new times and new condi-

---

1. Canon 762, §1; Canon 793; Canon 824, §1.

tions. It is but logical, then, from the very outset of this treatise dealing with the ceremonial office of sponsor, to direct attention and investigation to those early ages of Christianity, when the Church began to clothe the administration of Christ's sacraments in the glorious and brilliant cloak of her ritual. In fact, the Church herself directs attention to practices of early Christian times by prefacing the legislation pertaining to sponsors with the words, "*Ex vestustissimo more Ecclesiae.*"[2] The plain statement of the obligation to have a sponsor at Baptism would have been quite sufficient for the purpose of the legislator. But as if to enhance the force of the precept, to indicate the acceptance it received among the Christians of former times, and to emphasize the antiquity of the institution, the words "*ex vestustissimo Ecclesiae more*" are used by way of introduction. Moreover, in attributing the use of sponsors at solemn Baptism to the ancient custom of the Church, the Code gives the judicial basis upon which this precept rests, namely, custom.

The time of their institution is lost in the dawn of Christian antiquity. There is no Scriptural warrant for their existence, yet as early as the second century, they are found functioning at solemn Baptism with the approval of Christian tradition.

The important place which custom held in the formation of the early discipline of the Church is not to be underestimated. The primitive Christian communities in many cases had been formed and instructed by the Apostles themselves, or by their immediate successors, and hence whatever recognized customs began, or obtained among them, must have received the approbation of the competent authority. In many instances, there was no codification of laws, or compilation of writ-

2. Canon 762, §1; Canon 793.

ten statutes to direct their actions. The content of Christian dogma and discipline had been in most cases orally communicated, and the conformable deportment of the faithful under the direction of their spiritual guides begot the habit of Christian conduct.

The importance that Baptism held in the life of the individual Christian would naturally lend itself to much ceremony. It was the sacrament of regeneration whereby he was ascribed to the fold of Christ. It was the salutory laver which cleansed the soul of the guilt of original sin; the heavenly boon that raised his soul by sanctifying grace to a participation of the divine nature. To have an external manifestation indicative of the tremendous spiritual transformation that was being effected seems quite befitting and appropriate. It would impress upon the recipient the dignity to which he was being elevated, and recall to the spectators of the ceremony the exalted station to which they had been inducted when they chose to accept and live the doctrine of Christ. Hence, it is not surprising that many customs grew around the ceremony of conferring Baptism in the early days, nor that many of them have continued till the present.

The sacred rites performed when the sacrament of Baptism is solemnly administered are as ancient as they are beautiful. The form for solemn Baptism prescribed in the Roman Ritual of the present, far from being encumbered with modern rites foreign to ancient simplicity, is but a brief compendium of the solemn ceremonial of the early Christians. From the writings of the Fathers of the Church and the ancient liturgies, one learns that many of these ceremonies, if not actually founded in Apostolic practice, are based on the custom and practice of the first Christian communities. A comparison of the present baptismal ceremony, and that of the early Church, will demonstrate the antiquity of these solemn rites. Moreover, an explanation of the ancient and modern baptismal ceremony would afford one a better understanding and a clearer comprehension concerning the developments of the ecclesiastical laws and regulations regarding the use of sponsors, the qualifications demanded of those who would act in this capacity, and the terms used to designate those who functioned in this office. The important role which the sponsor acted in the ceremony will at once be apparent.

Observe the order prescribed by the Roman Ritual for the baptism of infants.[3] The child is brought by the sponsors to the door of the Church where it is met by the priest. They do not immediately enter the Church with the child, for, strictly speaking, the unbaptized are forbidden to enter the Church, because being subject to diabolical servitude by reason of original sin, they are not yet considered worthy to enter the temple of the Lord, wherein dwell only the children of the family of Christ.[4] After the godparents, in the name of the child, have asked for the gift of faith from the Church of God, the priest breathes upon the infant's face, and exorcises the evil spirit. Saint Augustine speaks of this Apostolic practice of exorcising to prove the existence of original sin, and the subjection of the unbaptized to diabolical influence.[5] Then the infant's forehead and breast are signed with the cross. This is one of the most ancient ceremonies by which one was admitted to the ranks of the Catechumenate.

Next follows the imposition of hands, another ceremony of admission to the Catechumenate, and a custom dating back to Apostolic practice. A few grains of salt are then placed in the mouth of the child to signify that he who is delivered from the corruption of sin by

---

3. *Rituale Romanum*, tit II, cap 2.
4. Pesch, "*Praelectiones Dogmaticae*," tom VI, n. 481.
5. *De peccatorum meritis et remissione*, lib I, c. 34, MPL XLIV, 146.

the doctrine of faith, and by the gift of grace, should experience a relish for good works, and be delighted with the food of divine wisdom.[6]

Placing his stole over the child the priest leads it into the Church, where on the way to the baptismal font the sponsors on the child's behalf make a profession of faith. Arrived at the font, the priest touches the ears and nostrils of the child with spittle, after the example of Christ, Who after having spread clay over the eyes of the blind man mentioned in the Gospels, commanded him to wash them in the Pool of Siloe and thus restored his sight, so the efficacy of the sacred ablution is such as to bring light to the mind to discern heavenly truth.[7] The child, through his sponsors, then makes a triple renunciation of Satan, and all his works and pomps, and is anointed with the oil of catechumens on the breast and between the shoulders. After this, the sponsors in the child's name make a profession of faith, and ask for Baptism. The priest then baptizes the child, and during the ablution the sponsors either hold, or at least touch the child, or receive it immediately from the priest after the sacramental ablution. After the Baptism, the crown of the child's head is anointed with chrism, and a white garment or veil is put on him, with the prayer, "Receive this white garment which mayest thou carry without stain before the judgment seat of our Lord Jesus Christ, that thou mayest have eternal life, Amen." Then the newly baptized is given a lighted candle by the priest, with the admonition: "Receive this burning light and keep thy Baptism so as to be without blame. Observe the commandments of God; that when Our Lord shall come to His nuptials, thou mayest meet Him together with all the Saints, and mayest have life ever-

6. *Catechismus Concilii Tridentini*, cap II, n. 66.
7. *Catechismus Concilii Tridentini*, cap II, n. 68.

lasting, and live forever and ever, Amen." The new Christian is then bidden to go in peace.

It will be noted that it is the sponsors who present the infant at the Church, who in its name ask for the gift of faith, make the profession of faith and the renunciation of Satan, and who perform practically all the functions of which the child is incapable.

In the baptism of adults, all the essential ceremonies are the same as for infants. However, the ritual prescribes that when the candidate for baptism is an adult, he should be well instructed in Christian faith and morals, and for some days prior to his Baptism should have given sufficient indication by his good conduct of his firm resolve to receive and abide in the mode of Christian living which Baptism enjoins.[8] Moreover, the candidate is to personally reply to the interrogations of the minister and to make the renunciation of Satan, the profession of faith, and the petition for Baptism. If, through some impediments, he is unable to do so, this deficiency is to be supplied by the sponsor.[9]

The order followed in the Baptism of adults,[10] though practically the same as that used in baptizing children, makes some impressive additions. The minister of the sacrament wears a cope over his other vestments and should be attended by at least two clerics. While the candidate waits outside the church door, the minister recites some prayers at the altar. Then he proceeds to the place where the candidate awaits, and asks him the questions concerning the gift of faith, the renunciation of Satan, and belief in the principal articles of the Faith. An explicit renunciation of the form of error to which the candidate had formerly adhered is made, and he is then signed with the cross on the brow, ears, eyes,

8. Canon 752, §1; *Rituale Romanum*, tit II, cap 3, n. 1.
9. *Rituale Romanum*, tit II, cap 3, n. 7.
10. *Rituale Romanum*, tit II, cap 4.

nostrils, mouth, breast and between the shoulders. After this on bended knees the candidate recites the Lord's Prayer, at the conclusion of which he is bidden by the minister to arise. He is then signed on the forehead by his sponsor, then by the minister, who taking him by the hand, leads him into the Church, where prostrating, he adores, and then rising recites the Apostles' Creed and the Lord's Prayer. The remaining ceremonies are practically the same as for infants. The ritual subjoins, however, that if a bishop be present who may legitimately confer confirmation on the newly baptized, it should be then administered;[11] and if the time be opportune, Mass should be celebrated at which the Neophytes are to assist and receive Holy Communion.[12]

The present ceremonial for Baptism, whether for children or adults, can be distinguished in three different parts; namely, the ceremonies that precede the baptismal ablution; secondly, the rites concurrent with the actual administration, or conferring of the sacrament; and finally those ceremonies which are performed after the Baptism has been conferred. This distinction has its foundation in the practice of the early Church, when these different ceremonies were performed at given intervals. The ceremonies preceding Baptism are reminiscent of the rites which accompanied one's admission to the Catechumenate in the early days of Christianity, and of the other ceremonies which marked the candidate's preparation and progress towards that condition of fitness required at Baptism. At the completion of the Catechumenate, the actual Baptism with its own proper ceremonial took place. Later followed a group of ceremonies indicating the Christian dignity and spiritual purity of the newly baptized. In all these ceremonies, the sponsor played an important

11. *Rituale Romanum*, tit II, cap 4, n. 56.
12. Canon 753.

part, much as he does at the present time. An explanation, therefore, of the development and practice of the ancient baptismal ceremonial, and of the rites and ceremonies relating to it would seem opportune.

In the commission of Our Divine Master to His Apostles, Christ said to them, "All power is given to me in heaven and in earth. Going, therefore, teach ye all nations, baptizing them in the name of the Father, and of the Son and of the Holy Ghost. Teaching them to observe all things whatsoever I have commanded you. And behold I am with you all days even to the consummation of the world."[13] The divine command embraced a two-fold obligation, to teach and to baptize. It was by teaching that the Apostles were to bring followers to Christ. The Gospel was to be made known to all peoples. All things whatsoever Christ had delivered to the Apostles, and the Apostles to the Church, were to be taught and explained according to the capacity of their audiences. The Divinity of Jesus Christ, our Lord and Redeemer, must be explicitly professed. "This is eternal life: that they may know Thee, the only true God, and Jesus Christ whom Thou hast sent."[14] "He that believeth in the Son, hath life everlasting; but he that believeth not the Son shall not see life, but the wrath of God abideth on him."[15]

In obedience to Christ's command, Saint Peter, "standing up with the eleven," declared to the Jews on the first Pentecost day, and proved to them from the Scriptures that Jesus, whom they had crucified, was "Lord and Christ." When they had been convinced of this truth and had compunction in their hearts for their sins, they asked, "What shall we do?" Peter answered, "Do penance; and be baptized every one of you in the

---

13. Matthew XXVIII, 18-20.
14. John XVII, 3.
15. John III, 36.

name of Jesus Christ, for the remission of your sins." "They, therefore, that received his word were baptized, and there were added in that day about three thousand souls."[16] So, too, at Caesarea, it was after a brief instruction in fundamentals of the Christian doctrine that Peter baptized Cornelius and the people of that place who had accepted Peter's teaching.[17] It seems to have been the Apostolic practice that some sort of preliminary instruction was always given to converts before their Baptism. Philip instructed the eunuch and the Samaritans before baptizing them.[18] The instruction of Theophilus was probably, at least in part, before Baptism.[19] Lydia's Baptism was followed by a preaching,[20] as was that of the Corinthians.[21]

In the Apostolic times we never read of any long interval between the time of a person's first conversion and his Baptism. The history of the Jews at Jerusalem on the first Pentecost, of Cornelius, and the Ethiopian eunuch, of the jailer of Philippi, and others mentioned in the Acts of the Apostles, are sufficient evidence that in those days catechizing, or instruction, and Baptism immediately accompanied one another. Later, however, the Church found it necessary to lengthen this prebaptismal period of instruction and probation, lest an overhasty admission of persons to Baptism should either fill its membership with unworthy people, or make a greater number of renegades and apostates in time of persecution.

It was this danger of apostasy, and betrayal in time of persecution, which gave rise to special precautions in admitting candidates to the Church. To avert this danger, a careful intellectual and moral preparation was

---

16. Acts II, 2-41.
17. Acts X, 1-48.
18. Acts VIII, 5-35.
19. Luke I, 4.
20. Acts XVI, 13.
21. Acts XVIII, 5.

needed; intellectual, to guard against the arguments of the pagan philosophers; moral, to give strength against the torments of the persecutors. Hence, we find in the early ages of the Church, the Catechumenate, which was the name applied to that class of candidates for Baptism, who had not yet been initiated into the sacred mysteries, but were undergoing a course of preparation for that purpose.

If a pagan wished to become a Christian he was given some elementary instruction in the fundamental doctrines and practices of the Church. He had to show by his conduct that he was in earnest as to the step he was about to take. So far, he was only in the stage of inquiry, and was not counted as a Christian. As soon as his instructors were satisfied that he was likely to persevere, the enquirer was promoted to the rank of catechumen. By virtue of his admission to this state, the catechumen had some title to the common name of Christian. He was considered above heretics or infidels, but not yet enjoying the full rights of a Christian.

The admission to the Catechumenate was accompanied by some ceremony. In the early ages the rites of admission to the Catechumenate were quite simple, but in course of time became more elaborate.[22] At first the candidates were merely signed on the forehead with the sign of the cross or hands imposed upon them with suitable prayers, and sometimes both ceremonies were used.[23] Thus St. Augustine, in his model of instruction to an enquirer, says: "He should be asked whether he believes what he has heard and is ready to observe it. If he answers in the affirmative he should be solemnly signed and treated according to the manner of the Church."[24] Eusebius, speaking of Constantine's prayers

22. Martene, "*De Antiquis Ritibus*," lib I, cap 1, art VI, nn. 4-18, "*Ordines ad faciendum catechumenum.*"
23. Martene, "*De Antiquis Ritibus*," lib I, cap 1, art IV, n. 4.
24. *De Catechizandis Rudibus*, MPL XL, 344.

in the Church at Helenopolis a little before the time of the Emperor's death, says that it was in the same Church where Constantine had been first admitted to the imposition of hands and prayer, that is, had been made a Catechumen by these ceremonies.[25]

Different authors and historians enumerate various classes of Catechumens; some have a general division of two classes, others have as many as fifteen separate groups. It may be well for the sake of clarity to disregard the contentions of these various writers regarding the exact number of degrees in the Catechumenate and follow a division proposed by one author.[26]

The lowest degree of Catechumens included those who were privately instructed, that is to say, not in the Church, and those who prior to their Baptism had committed some delinquency, and by ecclesiastical penalties were not allowed to enter the Church and thus were reduced to the lowest rank of the Catechumenate in punishment for their fault.[27]

The next degree, or second class of Catechumens were hearers or *audientes*. These were so called because they were admitted to hear sermons, and the Scriptures read in the Church, but not allowed to remain for any of the prayers. Immediately after the sermon a deacon solemnly announced, "*Ne quis audientium adsit,*" whereupon the *audientes* left the Church.[28]

The third degree was known as the kneelers or prostrators, or *genuflectentes*. This class of Catechumens might not only hear sermons but also attend some particular prayers of the Church that were especially offered up for them whilst they were on their knees, waiting for the imposition of hands and the minister's benediction.[29]

25. "*Vita Constantini,*" cap IV, n. 61, MPG XX, 1213.
26. Bingham, "*Antiquities of the Christian Church,*" lib X, cap 2.
27. Bingham, "*Antiquities of the Christian Church,*" lib X, cap 2, n. 2.
28. Bingham, "*Antiquities of the Christian Church,*" lib X, cap 2, n. 3.
29. Bingham, "*Antiquities of the Christian Church,*" lib X, cap 2, n. 4.

The fourth order of Catechumens were the *competentes* and *electi.* These terms were used to denote the immediate candidates for Baptism, or such as had given their names to the bishops, signifying their desire to be baptized on the next approaching festival. Their petitioning of this favor gave them the name of *competentes;* and from the bishop's examination and approbation, or choice of them, they were styled *electi.*[30]

When the names of the *competentes* or candidates for Baptism had been submitted and their petition accepted, the name of the candidate and that of his sponsor were registered in the books of the Church.[31] After their names had been registered, the candidates were subjected to several examinations to determine their knowledge of the Christian Doctrine in which they had been instructed, and their general fitness to receive Baptism.[32]

The instructions given to a Catechumen comprised the common principles of religion, the doctrine of the remission of sins, the necessity of prayer and good works, the nature, necessity and use of Baptism, by which the Catechumen was taught how to renounce the evil spirit and his works, and enter into a new covenant with God. This was followed by an explanation of the articles of the Apostles' Creed; the nature and immortality of the soul, and some discourses in the Scripture. An excellent example of the Catechumen instruction is afforded by the discourses of St. Cyril to the Catechumens.[33]

---

30. Bingham, "*Antiquities of the Christian Church,*" lib X, cap 2, n. 5.
31. Bingham, "*Antiquities of the Christian Church,*" lib X, cap 2, n. 6.
32. Bingham, "*Antiquities of the Christian Church,*" lib X, cap 2, n. 7.
33. "*Catecheses,*" MPG XXXIII, 369 sqq. Other early examples of catechetical instruction are found in St. Justin, "*Apologia I,*" MPG VI, 328 sqq.; Tertullian, "*De Baptismo,*" MPL I, 1197 sqq.; St. Augustine, "*De Catechizandis Rudibus,*" MPL XL, 309 sqq.; "*Sermones ad Competentes LVI-LIX,*" MPL XXXVIII, 377 sqq.; "*In Traditione et Redditione Symboli,*" MPL XXXVIII, 1058 sqq.

There were usually seven examinations, or scrutinies, given a Catechumen. Three of them were made on the Monday, Wednesday and Saturday of the third week of Lent. Three others on the same days of the fourth week, and the last on Easter Saturday, immediately before the Baptism. The questions which the priest now puts to the candidates are taken from this ancient form of scrutiny, and are directed to ascertain the object had in view by the candidate, which should be no other than his eternal salvation. "What doth thou ask of the Church of God?" "Faith." What does Faith bring to thee?" "Life everlasting." The questions concerning the renunciation of Satan, a belief in the Three Divine Persons, and in the Holy Catholic Church, were proposed in the ancient scrutinies in the precise terms used today. They were repeated at each scrutiny, the better to test the sincerity and fixed resolution of the Catechumen.[34]

The sponsor's attestation to the good intentions of the baptismal candidate are precisely to strengthen the assurance required by the Church, that these scrutinies had been answered truthfully and sincerely. Hence, the purpose of repeating these scrutinies, or examinations, is the same object which the Church has in view in the use of sponsors, at least in the case of adults.

Although in cases of necessity Baptism might be conferred at any time,[35] still, the usual and almost general practice of the ancient Church was to administer Baptism on the solemn festivals of Easter and Pentecost.[36] Before the churches and baptisteries were built, Baptism was conferred in any place which was convenient. Tertullian observes that St. Peter baptized his converts in the Tiber at Rome, as John had done in the Jor-

---

34. Kenrick, "*Treatise on Baptism,*" p. 203.
35. C. 16, D. IV, de cons.
36. C. 12, 13, 14, 15, 17, 18, D. IV, de cons.

dan; nor did it make any difference as far as validity of the sacrament was concerned, whether a man was baptized in the sea, or in a lake, or river, or stream.[37] In after ages, however, when baptisteries were built adjoining the Church, Baptism was ordinarily administered nowhere but in them, except by explicit dispensation of the local bishop.[38]

The periods of the Catechumenate being completed, the candidate was then presented for Baptism. The candidate, before entering the baptismal font, or pool, made a solemn profession of the Christian faith in the words prescribed by the Church's ritual.[39] Then, in the presence of the assembled congregation, and kneeling under the imposed hands of the minister of the sacrament, the candidate made a solemn renunciation of the devil and all his pomp. Thereupon the candidate was thrice immersed, and made a promise to live in obedience to the laws of Christ and his Church.[40]

Immediately after the neophyte emerged from the water, he was clothed in a white garment which was worn by him for eight days following.[41] The newly baptized were also given lighted tapers to carry.[42] Another ceremony used to congratulate those just baptized upon their admission and incorporation into the Church, was the kiss of peace with which the Christian brethren saluted the newly inducted member.[43] The neophytes were also given a taste of milk and honey, which was the food commonly given to babies, to signify

---

37. "*De Baptismo,*" cap IV, MPL I, 1204.
38. Bingham, "*Antiquities of the Christian Church,*" lib XI, cap VI, nn. 11-13.
39. Tertullian, "*De Spectaoulis,*" cap IV, MPL I, 635.
40. Tertullian, "*De corona militis,*" cap III, MPL I, 78-79.
41. Martene, "*De Antiquis Ritibus,*" lib I, art XV, n. 9; Bingham, "*Antiquities of the Christian Church,*" lib XII, cap IV, nn. 1-3.
42. Martene, "*De Antiquis Ritibus,*" lib I, art XV, n. 9; Bingham, "*Antiquities of the Christian Church,*" lib XII, cap 4, n. 4.
43. Martene, "*De Antiquis Ritibus,*" lib I, art XV, n. 1.

their re-birth in Christ.[44] They also received Holy Communion after the baptismal ceremony, nor was any distinction made whether the newly baptized was an infant or an adult.[45]

Confirmation was usually conferred immediately after the baptismal ceremony on both infants and adults.[46] The practice of conferring Confirmation and giving the Holy Eucharist immediately after Baptism to both infant and adult candidates, continued until the ninth century,[47] and in some places even as late as the eleventh century.[48]

Besides the ceremonies enumerated above, it was the practice in some early communities after Baptism to place a wreath on the head of the newly baptized and also to wash his feet.[49] The participation of the sponsors in the ancient ceremony, when the candidates presented were infants, was to make the renunciation of Satan, the profession of faith, and in general, perform all the requisites for solemn Baptism of which the child was incapable. In the Baptism of adults the sponsor gave added assurance of the baptismal promises of their spiritual protégé, having previously taken care to see that the candidate had been sufficiently instructed in Christian Doctrine, and manifested by his conduct a serious resolve and purpose toward the Christian dignity with which he was to be honored. The sponsor also held his god-child during the baptismal ablution, or assisted him to emerge from the saving waters, and clothed him in the ceremonial white garment after the Baptism. It is with good reason, therefore, that the Code introduces

44. Martene, "*De Antiquis Ritibus,*" lib I, art XV, n. 16.
45. Martene, "*De Antiquis Ritibus,*" lib I, art XV, n. 11; Bingham, "*Antiquities of the Christian Church,*" lib XII, cap IV, n. 9.
46. Martene, "*De Antiquis Ritibus,*" lib I, art XV, n. 11; Bingham, "*Antiquities of the Christian Church,*" lib XII, cap 1, nn. 1-2.
47. Bingham, "*Antiquities of the Christian Church,*" lib XII, cap IV, n. 9.
48. Martene, "*De Antiquis Ritibus,*" lib I, art XV, n. 13.
49. Martene, "*De Antiquis Ritibus,*" lib I, art XV, nn. 7-8.

the legislation relating to sponsors with a suggestion to their antiquity.

According to the very ancient custom and practice of the Church, which continued to obtain down through the ages, no one should be solemnly baptized unless he has, insofar as it is possible, his own sponsor. This legislation of the Church is expressed in canon 762, §1 of the Code, which reads: *"Ex vetusissimo Ecclesiae more nemo sollemniter baptizetur, nisi suum habeat, quatenus fieri possit, patrinum."*

The words *"solemniter baptizetur,"* referring to solemn Baptism are used in contradiction to private Baptism. Solemn Baptism is that conferring of the sacrament in which all the rites and ceremonies prescribed by the ritual are employed; otherwise, the Baptism is considered private. This distinction is expressed in the Code, under canon 737, §2: *"Cum ministratur (Baptismus) servatis omnibus ritibus et caeremoniis quae in ritualibus libris praecipiuntur appellatur sollemnis; secus, non sollemnis, seu privatus.* The words *"omnibus ritibus et caeremoniis,"* however, do not mean that if one or more of the ceremonies prescribed for solemn Baptism are omitted, whether through necessity, or negligence, that the Baptism is not to be considered as solemn Baptism. This may be deduced from an instruction given on September 15, 1869, by the Holy Office, in response to an inquiry whether, in case of necessity, namely, where there were no other capable or suitable persons to be had who could act as sponsors, it would be lawful to have the parents materially, not formally, function in the capacity of sponsors for their own children, or whether in such a case, it would be better to confer the baptism privately, or without ceremony.

The response of the Congregation began by distinguishing between solemn and private Baptism. *"Porro quaestionis ratio postulat, ut praenotetur dis-*

crimen sollemnis a privato Baptismate; ex eo enim facile inferri poterit, an solus patrini defectus postulet quod solemni privatus subrogetur. Privatus igitur Baptismus, ut probe noscis, ille dicitur, in quo nulla alia caeremonia a Rituali praescripta adhibetur nisi ablutio baptizandi, verbis formae prolatis, iis videlicet quae Baptismo jure divino necessaria sunt. Sollemnis vero censetur quando ii quoque adhibentur ritus ac caeremoniae, quas Rituale Romanum memorat acceptas et approbatas ab apostolica et antiquissima traditione fuisse, et ad ejus sollemnitatem pertinere. Jam vero relate ad usum rituum istorum Rituale ipsum admonet eos haud licere omittere, nisi causa necessitatis; quod quidem eadem S. C. (i. e. Sancti Officii) oraculo suo confirmavit. Cum enim quaesitum fuerit anno 1663: *'An in locis ubi non adest ecclesia parochialis, neque fons baptismalis conferri possit baptisma cum omnibus solemnitatibus et caeremoniis Ecclesiae consuetis;' decreto feriae IV,* 28 *Febr. praedicti anni praescriptum fuit, 'quod possint, immo teneantur uti illis caeremoniis, quibus possint uti.' Quare liquet illico privatum solemni Baptismo substituendum non esse, eo quod aliqua fieri nequeat caeremonia, nam, hac omissa, ceterae adimplendae sunt.*"[50]

The obligation to have a sponsor in solemn Baptism is *sub gravi,* unless a sufficiently grave and reasonable cause is present to excuse from it.[51] The Council of Trent strongly urges the fulfillment of this precept in directing the pastors to make inquiries before the time appointed for the baptismal ceremony, who are to act as the sponsors; *Officium parochi est, antequam ad Baptismum conferendum accedat, diligenter ab iis ad quos spectat, sciscitari quem vel quos elegerint, ut baptizatum*

50. Collectanea S. C. de Prop. Fide, n. 1347.
51. Gury-Ballerini, "*Theologia Moralis,*" vol II, n. 250; Genicot-Salsmans, "*Institutiones Theologiae Moralis,*" vol II, n. 156; Cappello, "*De Sacramentis,*" vol I, n. 181.

de Sacro Fonte suscipiant."[52] The Roman Ritual contains the same admonition.[53]

This obligation to supply a suitable and capable sponsor is primarily incumbent on the parents, or guardians, in cases where their children are to be baptized. But, if these people failed in this obligation, it would seem obligatory on the pastor, if, of course, it were possible for him to do so, to supply a sponsor for the child. In the case of an adult candidate for Baptism, he should be told of the obligation of having a sponsor, and be directed to have someone suitable act for him in that capacity.

Even in private Baptism, if a sponsor can be easily had, he should be employed; if, however, a sponsor cannot be obtained without serious inconvenience, the private Baptism may be performed without a sponsor. Later, however, when the solemn ceremonies are supplied, there should be a sponsor, but in this case no spiritual relationship is contracted. This legislation is contained in §2 of canon 762, "*Etiam in baptismo privato patrinus, si facile haberi queat, adhibeatur; si non interfuerit, adhibeatur in supplendis baptismi caeremoniis sed hoc in casu nullam contrahit spiritualem cognationem.*"

Ordinarily, Baptism should be conferred solemnly;[54] however, when there is danger of death, or in the case of adult heretics who are to be conditionally baptized, the Baptism may be given privately.[55]

The Code now imposes the obligation of having a sponsor at private Baptism. The force of this obligation, however, does not seem to be as strict as that contained in the first paragraph of this canon. In demanding a sponsor for solemn Baptism we have the words "*qua-*

52. Sess. XXIV, cap 2, *de reformatione matrimonii.*
53. Tit II, cap I, n. 22.
54. Canon 755, §1.
55. Canon 759, §1-2.

tenus fieri possit," which postulates a grave and serious reason to excuse from it; the wording of §2, however, "*si facile haberi queat,"* seems to admit of reasonable, even though slight, cause as excuse from having a sponsor at private Baptism.[56]

This precept of having a sponsor at private Baptism is a change from the old law. Formerly, it was considered as a laudable practice to have sponsors at private Baptism, but by no means preceptive.[57] The new law, however, makes it obligatory to have a sponsor at private Baptism, but allows a less cogent reason for dispensing with the sponsor, than at solemn Baptism. Even though there is no person capable or suitable to be had to act in this capacity at private Baptism, there should be one or two witnesses present to attest to the valid conferring of the sacrament, if it be possible to have such.[58] The distinction between private and solemn Baptism has been emphasized because in the law prior to the Code there was some dispute regarding the spiritual relationship arising from private Baptism. All the doctors agreed that in private Baptism the minister of the sacrament contracted spiritual relationship with the one baptized, but whether the sponsors also contracted spiritual relationship was much disputed.[59]

---

56. Cappello, "*De Sacramentis,*" vol I, n. 182.
57. St. Alphonsus, "*Theologia Moralis,*" lib VI, n. 147.
58. Canon 742, §1.
59. Cf. St. Alphonsus,"*Theologia Moralis,*" lib VI, n. 149; Sanchez, "*De Matrimonio,*" lib VII, disp LXII, n. 14; Reiffenstuel, "*Jus Canonicum Universum,*" lib IV, tit XI, n. 14; Schmalzgrueber, "*Jus Ecclesiasticum Universum,*" lib IV, tit XI, n. 55; Gasparri, "*De Matrimonio,*" vol I, n. 836; Wernz, "*Jus Decretalium,*" tomus IV, n. 489.

CHAPTER II

The Origin of Baptismal Sponsors

Among the early customs that are found in the ancient baptismal ceremony was that of having a sponsor for the newly baptized. At precisely what time this function or office originated, is difficult to say. Many writers have set forth different explanations to account for the origin of this custom.

According to Corblet, in his work, "*Histoire du Sacrement de Baptême,*" some Protestant writers would have us accept the theory that the employment of sponsors at Christian Baptism is derived from a practice in Roman law. They base their explanation on the fact that just as the Roman law postulated the presence of two witnesses to attest to the validity of a contract, so, too, they say, Baptism was a sort of initiation ceremony or contract by which one became affiliated to, or inducted into the membership of the Church, and hence, in this religious contract, witnesses were used in a similar capacity. This tendency to reduce the office of baptismal sponsor to the mere formality of witness is quite modern.[1]

Andre Schuler, in his treatise, "*De Susceptoribus ex Historia Ecclesiastica,*" would trace the origin of Christian sponsors at Baptism, as a custom growing out of, and conforming to the ceremony of circumcision in the Jewish Ritual, in which two witnesses were used; or to the procedure followed by the Jews in the baptism of proselytes.[2] This explanation seems to lose force

1. Corblet, "*Histoire du Sacrement de Bapteme,*" lib XII, cap 1.
2. Schuler, "*De Susceptoribus,*" cap IV.

when one considers that the early Church practice was to use only one sponsor in its baptismal ceremony, and not two; and the second hypothesis is untenable, because it cannot be shown that the baptism of proselytes in the Jewish religion is anterior to the introduction of Christianity.

The work of Vicecomes, "*Observationes Ecclesiasticae de Antiquis Baptismi Ritibus ac Caeremoniis,*" goes into the subject very thoroughly, and the author agrees with the opinion of one Ludolph, a Carthusian of Saxony, who contends that the custom of having sponsors is found in the time of the Gospels, and has perdured since then. Vicecomes writes, "*Majorem difficultatem habet quaestio unde in Ecclesiam susceptorum mos profectus fuerit. Cui ego sic occurro, ut ab illo Evangelii 'Et adduxit eum ad Jesum' ad nos manasse, existimem. Testimonio est Ludolphi Saxonis Carthusiani, locus, lib. I,' 'Vitae Christi,' cap.* 24.—"*Et adduxit eum ad Jesum*"—*ex hoc accepit Ecclesia quod in sacramento Baptismi et Confirmationis utitur Adducentibus, qui praesentent suscipientes Sacramentum, qui Patrini solent vocari.*"—*quae verba adeo manifesta sunt ut aliis testimoniis confirmare opus non sit.*"[3]

A number of other writers, among whom are Polydorus Virgilius, Hildebrand, Schubart, Gerhard, *et al.*, attribute the institution of the canonical and liturgical office of baptismal sponsor to Pope Hyginus, whose pontificate was in the middle of the second century.[4] They found their reasons on the fact that in the Decree of Gratian—§III. *De consec,* Dist. IV, can. 100—the legislation of this canon is attributed to that pontiff. The canon reads, "*Necessitate cogente in catecismo et confirmatione idem conpater esse potest.*" The quota-

3. Vicecomes, "*Observationes de antiquis Baptismi ritibus,*" lib I, cap 30, q. 1, n. 3.
4. Corblet, "*Histoire du Sacrement de Bapteme,*" lib XII, cap 1.

tion under this caption ascribed to Pope Hyginus, is as follows, "*In catecumino, et in baptismo, et in confirmatione unus patrinus fieri potest, si necessitas cogit. Non est tamen consuetudo Romana, sed singuli per singulos suscipiunt.*" The use of the word *patrinus* at once suggests a doubt as to the authenticity of this passage, since this term did not come into use in reference to baptismal sponsors till a much later period.[5] Furthermore, this canon of Gratian, as Coustant points out,[6] was first incorporated into canonical legislation by Ivo, the celebrated canonist of Chartres, who wrote before Gratian's time. Ivo attributes this canon not to Pope Hyginus, but to the "*Penitential of Theodore,*" written by Theodore, the seventh Archbishop of Canterbury, who died about the year 690.

Some conclude, from a passage none too explicit, in the writings of Justin Martyr, that there were sponsors used at Baptism in his time. The presumption is, perhaps, justifiable, but hardly from the text that is alleged to substantiate it. Justin is telling of his own Baptism, and of the ceremonies which accompanied it. And he relates that this same ceremonial is used by him. The passage from Justin reads as follows, "*Quomodo autem nos Deo consecravimus per Christum, id quoque exponimus . . . Deinde eo ducuntur a nobis, ubi aqua est, et eodem regenerationis modo regenerantur quo et ipsi sumus regenerati . . . Super eo qui regenerari voluerit et peccatorum penitentiam egerit, parentis omnium et Domini Dei nomen pronuntiatur, atque hoc ipsum tantummodo appellamus, cum eum baptizandum ad lavacrum deducimus.*"[7] From the phrase "*ad lavacrum*

---

5. Du Cange, "*Glossarium ad Scriptores Mediae et Infimae Latinitatis,*" tom V, vox "*Patrinus.*"
6. Coustant, "*Epist. Rom. Pontificum,*" tom I, col. 64: "*Est autem ex Theodori Cantuariensis Poenitentiali,* cap IV, *non sine interpolatione compositum.*"
7. "*Apologia I,*" cap LXI, MPG, VI, 420-422.

deducimus, is concluded the office of sponsor. The context, however, seems to indicate that this phrase applies to the minister of the sacrament leading the candidate for Baptism to the sacred font.

Wilfridus Strabo, a writer of the ninth century, contends that the Baptism of infants was not practiced before the fourth century, or after Saint Augustine's time, and is of the opinion, moreover, that the origin of sponsors can be attributed to the practice at infant Baptism. In his writings, *"De Rebus Ecclesiasticis,"* Strabo proposes the following concerning the origin of sponsors: *"Notandum deinde primis temporibus, illis solummodo baptismi gratiam dari solitam, qui et corporis et mentis integritate jam ad hoc pervenerant, ut scire, et intelligere possent quid emolumenti in baptismo consequendum, quid confitendum, atque credendum, quid renatis in Christo postremo esset servandum. Refert siquidem Venerabilis Pater Augustinus de se ipso in libris Confessionum suarum, quod pene usque ad XXV annorum aetatem catechumenus perdurarit; et ea videlicit intentione, ut per hanc temporis moram de singulis edoctus ad eligendum quodlibet libero duceretur arbitrio . . . sed augescente divinae Religionis diligentia, intelligentes Christiani dogmatis amatores, peccatum Adae non solos eos tenere obnoxios, qui suis operibus praevaricationem auxerunt, sed etiam eos, qui sine suis commissis; quia secundum Psalmistam, 'in iniquitatibus concepti et nati sunt,' immunes a peccato esse non possunt . . . necessario parvuli baptizantur. Ex hac igitur occasione inventum est, ut Patrini, vel Matrinae adhibeantur suscepturi parvulos de lavacro, et pro eis respondeant omnia, quae ipsi per aetatis infirmitatem confiteri non possunt."*[8]

This hypothesis of denying the Baptism of infants in the early ages of the Church is not in keeping with

8. *"De Rebus Ecclesiasticis,"* cap XXVI, MPL, CXIV, 960.

the teaching of the Fathers on this subject. Origen, for instance, writes, "*Ecclesia ab Apostolis traditionem suscepit etiam parvulis baptismum dare. Sciebant enim illi, quibus secreta mysteriorum commissa sunt divinorum, quod essent in omnibus genuinae sordes peccati, quae per aquam et Spiritum Sanctum ablui deberent.*"[9] Another passage from the writings of the same apologist can be cited: "*Parvuli baptizantur in remissionem peccatorum. Quorum peccatorum? Vel quo tempore peccaverunt? Aut quomodo potest ulla lavacri in parvulis ratio subsistere, nisi juxta illum sensum de quo paulo ante diximus. Nullus a sorde, nec si unius diei quidem fuerit vita ejus super terram. Et quia per baptismi sacramentum nativitatis sordes deponuntur, propterea baptizantur et parvuli. Nisi enim quis renatus fuerit ex aqua et Spiritu, non potest intrare in regnum coelorum.*"[10] Numerous other quotations from the early Fathers might be cited to prove that infants received Baptism even in the first days of the Church,[11] and hence, though the opinion that sponsors originated from the ceremony at infant Baptism may be admitted, still, it cannot be conceded that the time of their origin was after the time of Saint Augustine.

Gerard von Mastrich, in his treatise, "*Schediasma de Susceptoribus Infantium ex Baptismo,*" is of the opinion that sponsors had been used in the early days of the Church at infant Baptism, and that towards the end of the fourth century, this practice was applied in the Baptism of adults.[12]

---

9. "*Epist. ad Romanos,*" lib V, n. 9, MPL XIV, 1047.
10. Origen, "*Homilia in Lucam,*" cap XIV, MPL, XIII, 943.
11. St. Augustine, "*Epist 166 ad Hieronymum,*" cap XXIII, MPL, XXXIII, 731; "*De peccatorum meritis et remissione,*" lib I, cap 26, MPL, XLIV, 131; St. Irenaeus, "*Adversus Haereses,*" lib. II, cap 22, MPG, VII, 784; St. John Chrysostom, "*Homilia XL in Genesim,*" MPG, LIII, 373; "*St. Gregory Nazianzus,*" Oratio XLIX, MPG, XXXVI, 399.
12. Von Mastrich, "*Schediasma de Susceptoribus,*" cap XIV.

In his *"Dissertatio de Susceptorum Baptismalium Origine,"* Isaac Jundt agrees with von Mastrich in that sponsors were used at Baptism from the earliest times, but differs with him in alleging the reason for their origin. Jundt believes that sponsors were employed in the first centuries at adult Baptism. They were, he says, Christians who presented the candidates for Baptism, and gave assurances for the good dispositions of the subject, and later this custom was applied as a liturgical office in the Baptism of infants.[13]

If one concedes that Dionysius the Areopagite, or perhaps better said, the pseudo Aeropagite, lived in the first century, a very early record of the existence of Baptismal sponsors can be had. In his *"De Hierarchia Ecclesiastica,"* he writes, *"Quod autem infantes quoque, qui per aetatem nequeunt intelligere divinae regenerationis sanctissimorumque divinae communionis mysteriorum participes fiant, videtur, ut inquis, hominibus profanis non immerito risu dignum, quod pontifices eos erudiant, qui nequeunt audire, sanctasque traditiones non intelligentibus frustra tradant; neque minus ridiculum est quod alii pro eis abrenuntiationes sacrasque professiones pronuntient . . . Verum tamen hac de re id quoque dicimus, quod Deiformes praeceptores nostri ab antiqua traditione acceptum nobis transcripserunt. Aiunt, enim, quod et verum est, infantes, si in lege sacra instituantur, ad sanctum animi statum perventuros esse omni errore liberos, et sine ullo impurae vitae periculo. Hoc enim cum in mentem venisset divinis nostris institutoribus, placuit, admitti pueros hoc sancto modo, ut oblati parvuli parentes naturales filium uni ex fidelibus tradant, qui praeclare in divinis rebus erudiat. Sub cujus deinceps cura fit, tamquam sub patre divino, sanctaeque salutis susceptore. Hunc itaque Antistes, sancte promittentem se puerum ad sanctam vitam infor-*

13. Jundt, *"Dissertatio de Susceptorum Origine,"* cap XI.

maturum, jubet profiteri abrenuntiationes, sacrasque professiones; non enim ut illi subsannatores aiunt, alium pro alio rebus divinis imbuit; neque enim sponsor dicit. Ego pro puero abrenuntiationes facio, sacrasve professiones, sed hoc modo puerum asserit renunciare ac profiteri; ac si dicat: Profiteor me huic puero, cum per aetatem intelligere poterit sacra, divinis meis institutionibus persuasurum, ut adversarius nuntium omnino remittat, et divina promissa profiteatur, et exsolvat. Nihil ergo, ut opinor, absurdum est, si ad divinum institutum puer adducitur, cum ducem ac sponsorem habeat, qui eum, et divinarum rerum scientia imbuat, et ab adversariis tutum custodiat. Porro Pontifex puerum consortem facit sacrorum mysteriorum, ut in eis educetur, neque agat vitam aliam, quam rem, quae divina semper spectet, et hujusmodi sancta communione proficiat, atque in his sacrum habitum possideat, et a susceptore deiformi studiose promoveatur."[14]

The time in which the works attributed to Dionysius were composed, and the exact identity of the writer himself, has been the subject of much controversy since the fifteenth century, and even continues to our own day. After much research, it is generally conceded that the writings of this individual are of no later date than the fourth, or early part of the fifth century. Hence, whatever evidence is deduced from them must be considered with due regard to the certain antiquity of the author.[15] The above quotation taken from the writings of Dionysius, however, supports the claim of the early existence of the office of baptismal sponsor in the Church.

There is positive and explicit testimony of the existence of sponsors at Baptism in the second century, and an implicit reference to the responsibilities and duties

14. "*De Hierarchia Ecclesiastica,*" lib II, cap 7, n. XI, MPG, III, 567.
15. *Catholic Encyclopedia,* vol V, p. 13, art: "*Dionysius Pseudo-Areopagite.*"

annexed to this office, in the treatise, "*De Baptismo,*" by Tertullian. He does not refer to the office of sponsor as something new, or recently introduced, but accepts it as an already existing custom. When Tertullian speaks of the persons to whom, and of the time when, Baptism is to be administered, he pleads for the delay of infant Baptism. For his reasons, he alleges the incapacity of the child to realize or appreciate the dignity with which the sacrament endows its recipients; nor should the sponsors of the child, he argues, be endangered by making promises on the child's behalf, since they are not certain of being able to fulfil these promises. The passage from Tertullian, which is probably the earliest explicit mention of baptismal sponsors, reads as follows: "*Pro cujusque personae conditione ac dispositione, etiam aetate, cunctatio baptismi utilior est, praecipue tamen circa parvulos. Quid enim necesse est sponsores etiam periculo ingeri? Quia et ipsi per mortalitatem destituere promissiones suas possint, et proventu malae indolis falli. Ait quidem Dominus, 'Nolite illos prohibere ad me venire.' Veniant ergo dum adolescunt, veniant dum discunt, dum quo veniunt docentur; fiant Christiani, dum Christum nosse potuerint.*"[16]

In the life of Saint Sebastian, given in the "*Bollandist Acta Sanctorum,*" there is an account given of the Saint acting as sponsor at the Baptism of some converts. "*Igitur omnes isti sexaginta octo a Sancto Polycarpo Presbytero baptizati, et a Sancto Sebastiano suscepti sunt; Feminarum autem matres factae sunt Beatrix et Lucina.*"[17]

Rufinus Tyrannius, better known as Rufinus of Aquilea, who lived from about the year 345 to 410, tells of his own Baptism in his "*Apologia in Hieronymum,*" where he writes, "*Ego et ipse* (*i. e., Hier-*

16. "*De Baptismo,*" cap XVIII, MPL, I, 1221.
17. Tomus II, Januarii, cap XI, n. 36, p. 270.

onymous), et omnes norunt, ante annos fere triginta, in Monasterio jam positus, per gratiam Baptismi regeneratus, signaculum fidei consecutus sum per sanctos viros Chromatium, Jovium, et Eusebium, opinatissimos et probatissimos Dei Episcopos; quorum alter tunc presbyter beatae memoriae Valeriani, alter Archdiaconus, alius Diaconus, simulque pater mihi, ac doctor Symboli fuit."[18] The explanation of this text is that Chromatius was a *presbyter* of the bishop Valerianus; Jovinus, an archdeacon, and Eusebius, a deacon who had instructed Rufinus during the period of preparation for Baptism, and had acted as his sponsor at the solemn ceremony.[19] That deacons exercised this office of Baptismal sponsor, is known from the Apostolic Constitutions which contain the following legislation, *"Virum suscipiat diaconus, mulierem vero diaconissa."*[20]

That the custom of having a baptismal sponsor was practiced in the days of Saint Augustine is quite apparent from the many references he makes to them.[21] It seems that during Saint Augustine's time, in most cases, parents were sponsors for their own children, since he speaks of parents in all ordinary cases offering their own children at Baptism, and making the proper responses for them. *"Quid est illud, quod quando ad baptismum offeruntur, parentes pro eis tamquam fideidictores respondent, et dicunt illos facere quod illa aetas cogitare non potest, aut si potest, occultum est? Interrogamus enim eos a quibus offeruntur, et dicimus; 'Credit in Deum?' De illa aetate quae utrum sit Deus ignorat, respondent; 'Credit.' Et ad cetera sic respondetur singula quae quaeruntur. Unde miror parentes in istis*

18. Rufinus, "*Apologia in Hieronymum,*" MPL, XXI, 543.
19. Trombelli, "*Tractatus de Sacramentis,*" tomus II, dissert. VI, q. 3, n. X.
20. Lib. III, cap 16; SS. Concilia, I, 321.
21. "*De Peccatorum Meritis et Remissione,*" lib I, cap 34, n. 63. MPL, XLIV, 146; "*Epistola ad Bonafacium,*" MPL, XXXIII, 359, sq.

rebus tam fidenter pro parvulo respondere, ut dicant eum tanta bona facere quae ad horam qua baptizatur, baptizator interrogat, tamen eadem hora si subjiciam, 'Erit castus qui baptizatur, aut non erit fur?' nescio utrum audet dicere aliquis, 'Aliquid horum erit, aut non erit,' sicut mihi sine dubitatone respondet quod credat in Deum.''[22]

In the above passage just cited, a certain Bishop Boniface requests of Saint Augustine the solution of some difficulties of a moral nature, concerning the questioning of the sponsors at Baptism. The specific purpose of Boniface's communication is to ascertain whether the sponsors are morally justified in making promises and assurances on the child's behalf. For, Boniface argues, the sponsors have no certain or positive knowledge that the children will fulfil the promises made in their name. With the solution of this difficulty, the present study is not directly concerned. But the point of interest is that Bishop Boniface acknowledges this practice of sponsors answering for children at Baptism is sanctioned by custom, though he is seeking a reason to justify the custom, for in conclusion, he says, "*Ad istas ergo questiones peto breviter respondere digneris, ita ut non mihi de consuetudine praescribas, sed rationem reddas.*"

That the parents, according to the common practice of the time, functioned as sponsors to their own offspring, can be deduced from this same letter of Saint Augustine to the Bishop Boniface. So general must have been this practice that Boniface was evidently of the opinion that only the parents of the child could act as sponsors for it. Saint Augustine, wishing to correct this false notion, wrote to Boniface, "*Illud autem nolo te fallat, ut existimes reatus vinculum ex Adam tractum,*

22. St. Augustine, "*Epist. ad Bonifacium,*" MPL, XXXIII, 363.

aliter non posse disrumpi nisi parvuli ad percipiendam gratiam a parentibus offerantur."[23]

From what has been proposed in the preceding pages concerning the origin of sponsors, the claim of the early use of baptismal sponsors in the first ages of the Church seems justifiable. Tertullian refers to them as an already existing institution, as early as the second century. Other quotations prove that they continued to function in the centuries following. That the custom never fell into disuse, but continued to obtain to the present day, is apparent from the many laws and regulations that have been passed in every century from the sixth to the present pertaining to sponsors, and therefore presupposing their existence.

23. St. Augustine, "*Epist. ad Bonifacium,*" MPL, XXXIII, 362.

CHAPTER III

The Names of Sponsors

In the ordinary acceptance of the term a sponsor is one who takes upon himself the obligations of promising the satisfaction of a debt, or the fulfillment of a duty. Etymologically, the term takes its use from the Latin verb *spondere,* to promise.[1] From the earliest ages the Church has employed this office when she conferred the sacrament of Baptism or Confirmation upon any of her members.[2] Many different terms were used to designate the office of sponsor, but whatever the terminology, the Church always recognized an unvarying obligation on the part of the one assuming this office. The first mention found of the term "sponsor" is in Tertullian. *"Quid enim necesse est sponsores etiam periculo ingeri? Quia et ipsi per mortalitatem destituere promissiones suas possint, et proventu malae indolis falli."*[3]

It is quite possible that Tertullian borrowed this terminology from Roman Law, which had such terminology, and recognized in it the obligation analogous to the Christian obligations. The term *sponsio* in Roman Law was the name originally given to a contract concluded by a libation, that is a solemn vow or promise externalized and enhanced by the ritual of libation. The person thus vowing or promising emphasized his sincerity in the formula, "Even as this wine now flows, so may the punishing gods cause the blood of him to flow, who shall be the first to break this covenant." The

1. Century Dictionary—word "Sponsor," "godfather." Funk and Wagnalls, "Standard Dictionary," word "sponsor."
2. Canons 762, 793.
3. *"De Baptismo,"* cap XVIII, MPL, I, 1221.

obligation originally created by such a promise was purely moral or religious. It was not till later that the obligation assumed a legal character.[4] Whenever the term was employed by pagan authors it was never divorced from the idea of moral obligation, as is evidenced in the writings of Cicero, Livy, *et al.*[5]

With the advent of Christianity the term was taken over by ecclesiastical writers and accepted with practically the same connotation.[6] For the early Christian sponsors realized that they bound themselves to a moral obligation which was accentuated by their Christian faith. In the Baptism of adults the sponsor vouched for the good dispositions manifested by the candidate during the period of his catechumenate, and attested to the reliability of the candidate for the sacrament. The sponsor furthermore undertook to instruct the neophyte in the knowledge of the divine mysteries which were yet unknown to him, and bound himself in conscience to see to it that the newly baptized faithfully fulfilled his baptismal promises.

Those who thus obligated themselves, were from the nature of their office also called *Fideijussores* and *Fideidictores.*[7] These terms were also borrowed from Roman Law. They were applied to a contract of suretyship whereby a man bound himself to be personally answerable, that is, answerable with his own credit, for the debt of another as accessory debtor in addition to the person principally liable.[8] The Church was necessarily cautious in admitting new members to her ranks during the days of persecution. She realized that even the period of the Catechumenate was not always a sufficient guarantee of the sincerity, or of the future conduct

4. Sohn, "*Institutes of Roman Law,*" p. 64.
5. Cf. Freund-Leverett, "*Latin Lexicon,*" words "*Sponsio, sponsor, spondeo.*"
6. Dionysius, "*De Hierarchia Ecclesiastica,*" lib II, cap 7, n. XI, MPL, III, 567.
7. St. Augustine, "*Epist. ad Bonifacium,*" MPL, XXXIII, 359.
8. Sohm, "*Institutes of Roman Law,*" p. 384.

of the newly inducted member, and hence the testimony of the sponsor or *fideijussor* gave added assurance of the high character of the candidate.

Besides the terms mentioned above many other names were used to denote the office of sponsor. The underlying reason for the choice of these appellations, was the foreshowing of either physical action performed by the sponsor at the time of the ceremony, or of the spiritual relationship begotten and existing between the sponsor and the recipient of the sacrament. Hence we have the terms:

Susceptores, from the Latin "to receive," "to lift up in order to carry"—also, "To take under one's protection," which is indicative of both the physical act of lifting the child or receiving the adult from the sacred font, and of the spiritual tutelage to be exercised on behalf of the sponsor's spiritual pupil. *Levantes,* from the Latin "to lift," because in the Baptism of infants the sponsors lifted the child from the baptismal waters, or in the case of adults assisted the neophyte to arise after the immersion. *Gestantes,* from the Latin *gestare,* "to carry," because they carried in their arms the children whom they presented for the laving waters of the sacrament. The word *Tenentes* was applied to sponsors because they held in their arms the child to be baptized, or in the event when the candidate was an adult, they held the recipient of the sacrament by the shoulder to signify their voluntary acceptance of the office of sponsor in his behalf. *Adducentes, Traditores, Porrigentes, Afferentes, Offerentes* were other names indicative of like symbolism used to designate the presentation of a candidate for the sacrament by his sponsor.[9]

9. Trombelli, "*Tractatus de Sacramentis,*" tom I, sectione XVI, dis. VI, 2. 1; Corblet, "*Histoire du Sacrement de Bapteme,*" lib XII, art 1; Wernz, "*Jus Decretalium,*" tom IV, n. 485; Du Cange, *Glossarium ad Scriptores Infimae Latinitatis,*" voces "*Patrinus, matrina, sponsor.*"

Since one of the sponsors' principal duties was to initiate the neophyte in the truths of the Christian faith, they were called *Initiatores, Arbitri Initiationis, Duces Viae, Fidei Doctores, Fidgi Ductores, Deiformes Preceptores, Curatores, Nutricii, Profitentes, Promissores.*[10]

The more intimate and filial appellations of *Pater, Pater spiritualis, Pater divinus, Patres Lustrati, Patres Lustrici, Propatres, Patres Mystici, Pater in lavacro, Pater ex lavacro, Patrinus, Conpater,* and the correlative names of the feminine gender, such as *Mater, Mater Spiritualis, Commater, Matrina,* etc.,[11] arose from the idea of spiritual relationship which was begotten between the sponsor and his protégé in the spiritual regeneration.

The name used by the Code to signify a sponsor, whether of Baptism or Confirmation, is *Patrinus.* This term is perhaps the most apt and comprehensive to indicate this office. It is most generally regarded as a diminutive of *pater,* or a contraction of *pater divinus,*[12] which at once expresses the participation in the duties and obligations of the natural parent to his offspring, with the accompanying note that the fundamental, basic principle of this relationship is founded in something spiritual. This idea of the twofold relatonship of the sponsor has been perpetuated in the vernacular of nearly all the modern languages, for example, the English equivalent is "Godfather" and "Godmother;" the German, *Godsib,* that is, "parent in God;" the Italian *Padrino;* the Spanish, *Padrino, Madrina;* the Portuguese, *Padrinho,* and the French, *Parrain, Marrain.*

In their liturgical literature, the modern Greeks still use the expression *anadokos,* which is the equivalent of the Latin *susceptor,* but in common parlance speak of

---

10. Corblet, "*Histoire du Sacrement de Bapteme,*" lib XII, cap II, art I.
11. Corblet, "*Histoire du Sacr. de Bapt.,*" lib XII, cap 2, art I.
12. Du Cange, "*Glossarium ad Scriptores Infimae Latinitatis;*" vox, "Patrinus."

the office as *Kumpatros,* or the Latin *compater,* which is practically the same idea as "godfather," or the other analogous appellations cited above.[13]

The oldest use of the term *Patrinus,* according to Binterim,[14] is in the year 752. For authority, he cites Calmet's History of Lothair, which reads, "*Sanctissimus vir patrinus, seu spiritualis pater noster Willibrordus.*"[15]

---

13. Corblet, "*Histoire du Sacrement de Bapteme,*" lib XII, cap 2, art I, footnote n. 2, p. 178.
14. Binterim, Anton, "*Die Vorzueglichstein Denkwuerdigkeiten der Christ-Katholischen Kirche,*" vol I, p. 188.
15. "*Historia Lotharii,*" tom I, col. 273.

CHAPTER IV

The Number of Sponsors at the Baptismal Ceremony

The primitive function of baptismal sponsors in regard to adult candidates for Baptism seems to indicate that there was no obligation to have more than one sponsor, and that one to be of the same sex as the person to be baptized. This was, generally speaking, the universal custom of the ancient Church.[1]

The examples cited in the writings of the various hagiographers attest to this, but unfortunately, these indications are so rare that it would be rash to draw from them too general conclusions. It is, however, within the bounds of reason to state that the use of only one baptismal sponsor lasted till the fifth century, and some liturgists maintain that the custom of having a single godparent obtained till the ninth century.[2] There has been a great variety of usage regarding the number of sponsors at the baptismal ceremony, despite the ordinances of Councils and Synods which endeavored to establish in this matter a uniformity of practice.

Corblet is of the opinion that in the first five cenuries, there was only one sponsor, and that one a male, whether for persons of the male or female sex.[3] However, in the life of Saint Sebastian, there is recorded a baptismal ceremony at which two women, Lucine and Beatrice, acted as sponsors for a group of female converts,[4] and Saint Augustine tells of holy virgins of

1. Bingham, "*Antiquities of the Christian Church,*" lib XI, cap 8, n. 11.
2. Corblet, "*Histoire du Sacrement de Bapteme,*" lib XII, cap 7.
3. Corblet, "*Hist. du Sacr. de Bapt.,*" lib XII, cap 7.
4. Bollandista, "*Acta Sanctorum,*" tom II, Januarii, cap 11, n. 36, p. 270.

his day, who sponsored foundling children of either sex,[5] which seems to discredit this statement. However, continues Corblet, in the sixth century, a female was allowed to act as sponsor for girls, and towards the seventh and eighth centuries there came about a transition in favor of the use of one male and one female sponsor for every child. The reason alleged for this innovation was that the analogy between the natural and the spiritual generation might be the more emphatically effected.[6]

Prior to the Council of Metz, held in the year 888, there is no explicit ecclesiastical legislation regulating the number of sponsors that may, or should be used, at the baptismal ceremony. What the recognized practice prescribed must be deduced from the accounts we have of the early times, which refer to the conferring of the sacrament.

The texts in the Decree of Gratian, attributed to Pope Hyginus and Pope Leo the Great, which prescribe the use of only one sponsor at Baptism,[7] can hardly be accepted as authentic, since it has been shown that these passages are of much later date than the time when these Pontiffs lived.[8] The quotation attributed to Hyginus reads, "*In catecumino, et in baptismo, et in confirmatione unus patrinus fieri potest, si necessitas cogit. Non est tamen consuetudo Romana, sed singuli per singulos suscipiunt.*"[9] Coustant[10] has shown that this canon was first incorporated into canonical legislation by Ivo, the illustrious canonist of Chartres, who cites for its authority the "Penitential of Theodore," which was written by Theodore, the seventh Archbishop

5. "*Epist. ad Bonifacium,*" MPL, XXXIII, 362.
6. Corblet, "*Histoire Du Sacrement de Bapteme,*" lib XII, cap 7.
7. C. 100, D. IV, de cons.
8. Hyginus' pontificate was from the year 139 to 142; Leo's from 440 to 461.
9. C. 100, D. IV, de cons.
10. "*Epist. Rom. Pontificum,*" tom I, col 64E.

of Canterbury.[11] Whether Theodore had any earlier documentary authority for this statute is not clear, but there seems to be sufficient indication that custom sanctioned the use of only one sponsor in Theodore's time, for he says, "*Consuetudo Romana . . . singuli per singulos suscipiunt.*"

The restriction of having only one baptismal sponsor, attributed to Leo the Great, "*Non plures ad suscipiendum de Baptismo infantem accedant, quam unus, sive vir, sive mulier,*"[12] is also a disputed text. Trombelli discusses the authenticity of this quotation, and rejects it as spurious. "*Quae porro ex Leone Magno allegantur,*" he writes, "*Leonis Magni non sunt; atque id constat quidem ex eo, quod nullus profertur, aut proferri potest locus, ex quo desumpta sunt.*"[13]

However, the first document of incontestable date that can be alleged which explicitly ordains the use of only one sponsor at Baptism, and prohibits the employment of two or more, is the Council of Metz, held in 888. "*Et infantem nequaquam duo, vel plures, sed unus a fonte baptismatis suscipiat, quia in hujusmodi secta diabolo datur locus, et tanti ministerii vilescit. Nam unus Deus, unum Baptisma, unus qui a fonte suscipiat, debet esse pater vel mater infantis.*"[14] This legislation of Metz seems to be founded on the earlier practice in the Church, regarding the number of sponsors.

In the biography of Saint Sebastian, who lived in the third century, there is an account of a baptismal ceremony recorded, at which the Saint functioned as sponsor for a group of male converts, "*Igitur omnes isti sexaginta octo a Sancto Polycarpo Presbytero baptizati, et a Sancto Sebastiano suscepti sunt; Feminarum*

---

11. Theodore died in the year 690; cf. *Catholic Encyclopedia*, vol XIV, p. 571.
12. C. 101, D. IV, de cons.
13. Trombelli, "*Tractatus de Sacramentis,*" tom II, sect. XIV, q. VI.
14. C. 6; cf. SS. Concilia, IX, 414.

autem matres factae sunt Beatrix et Lucina."[15] Though this is only a single instance of the ceremony, it gives a reflection of the practice at this period.

So, too, in the fourth century, Rufinus of Aquilea tells of his own Baptism, at which a certain Eusebius who had instructed Rufinus in the truths of Christianity in preparation for Baptism, officiated as his sponsor at the solemn ceremony, "*Eusebius diaconus, simulque pater mihi, ac doctor Symboli fuit.*"[16] Again, in this baptismal ceremony of the fourth century, there is mention of only one sponsor.

In the Apostolic Constitutions, which were compiled not later than the end of the fourth century, or the beginning of the fifth,[17] there is an indication that only one sponsor was used, for these Constitutions prescribe, "*Ac virum suscipiat diaconus, mulierem vero diaconissa.*"[18] The use of the singular number, "*diaconus, diaconissa,*" in the wording of this statute would imply that only one sponsor assisted.

In the quotation from the writings of Dionysius, the Areopagite so-called, or pseudo Aeropagite, whose works are of no later date than the end of the fifth, or beginning of the sixth century,[19] it seems that only one sponsor was used at Baptism. For, in defending the practice of having baptismal sponsors, which some profane writers sought to ridicule, he writes, "*Hoc enim cum in mentem venisset divinis nostris institutoribus, placuit, admitti pueros hoc sancto modo, ut oblati parvuli parentes naturales filium UNI ex fidelibus tradant, qui praeclare in divinis rebus puerum erudiat.*"[20] The allu-

15. Bollandista, "*Acta Sanctorum,*" tom II, Januarii, cap XI, n. 36, p. 270.
16. "*Apologia in Hieronymum,*" MPL, XXI, 543.
17. "It is clear from internal evidence that the Apostolic Constitutions were compiled in Syria at the end of the fourth, or at the beginning of the fifth century;" Bardenhewer, "*Patrology,*" p. 350.
18. Lib III, cap 16; SS. Concilia, I, 321.
19. Bardenhewer, "*Patrology,*" p. 539.
20. "*De Hierarchia Ecclesiastica,*" lib II, cap 7, n. XI, MPG, III, 567.

sion of the natural parents entrusting the religious education of the child to one of the faithful, would suggest that there was only one. Moreover, throughout in referring to the baptismal sponsor he uses the singular number, "*Ego pro puero abrenuntiationes facio . . . Ac si sponsor dicat, Profiteor me huic puero . . . cum ducem ac sponsorem habeat qui eum divinarum rerum scientiarum imbuat . . . et a susceptore deiformi promoveatur.*"[21]

At the Baptism of Saint Epiphanius, the patriarch of Constantinople, who died in the year 535, there was only one sponsor, a certain Lucian. "*Post Evangelium itaque absolutum, ingressus Episcopus in baptisterium, et jussit Epiphanium ingredi, et ejus sororem, et cum ipsis Lucianum, qui etiam fuit pater ejus in sancto Baptismate.*"[22]

The wording in the civil statute enacted by Justinian about the year 530, which forbade the marriage of sponsor and godchild, seems to indicate the use of no more than one sponsor. "*Ea persona omnimodo ad nuptias venire prohibenda, quam aliquis, sive alumna, sive non, a sacrosancto suscepit baptismate . . .*"[23]

The wording of the instruction by Pope Nicholas to the Bulgarians, written in 866, would seem to imply that only one person was to function as baptismal sponsor, "*Qui diligere debet hominem qui se suscipiat de sacro fonte sicut patrem.*"[24]

From these individual instances of the baptismal ceremony and the conjectures based on the grammatical construction of earlier writings, which refer either directly or indirectly to baptismal sponsors, too general conclusions can not be drawn, but taken collectively, they

21. "*De Hierarchia Ecclesiastica,*" ibid.
22. Petavius, "*Opera Epiphanii,*" tom II, sect. VIII.
23. Cod. lib V, tit IV, de nuptiis, leg. 26.
24. C. 1, C. XXX, q. 3.

furnish some indication of the practice that obtained prior to the enactment of Metz in 888.

The legislation of Metz, restricting the use of only one sponsor, is reiterated in the Decree of Gratian.[25] Pope Boniface VIII writes that according to the canonical legislation, only one person ought to be admitted as baptismal sponsor. "*Quamvis non plures quam unus vir, vel una mulier accedere debeant ad suscipiendum de Baptismo infantem, juxta sacrorum canonum instituta; si tamen plures accesserint spiritualis cognatio inde contrahitur . . .*"[26]

About the thirteenth and the fourteenth centuries, the custom of having several baptismal sponsors was practiced in different localities of England, France and Germany. This is evidenced from the enactments of Synods and Provincial Councils of these countries, in their legislation concerning the number of persons that could, or should officiate. Most of these Councils ordained that there should be three sponsors. At the Baptism of a male child, there were to be two male sponsors, and one female. Two female sponsors and one male were to exercise this office at the Baptism of a female.

In Germany, the Councils of Trier and Mainz, held towards the end of the thirteenth century, permitted the use of three or four sponsors for the child at Baptism.[27]

The Council of Cologne, held in 1280, allowed three sponsors, but enjoined that persons related to the parents of the child, within the fourth degree of kindred, were not to be admitted to this office. "*Item duo vel tres tantum admittantur ad levandum puerum de bap-*

25. C. 100, D. IV, de cons.
26. C. 2, *de cognatione spirituali,* IV, 3 in VI.
27. Binterim, Anton, "*Die Vorzueglichsten Denkwerdigkeiten der Christ-Katholischen Kirche,*" vol. I, p. 194.

tismo, qui intra quartum gradum parentibus non sint juncti, nisi in necessitate."[28]

The Council of Canerich, held in 1300, permitted, but did not demand, the use of eight baptismal sponsors, four of whom were to be clerics, and four of the laity.[29]

In England, the Synod of Worcester, in the year 1240, prescribed that there should be at least three sponsors, but no more than three. "*Masculum ad minus duo masculi et una mulier suscipiant; feminam, duae mulieres et unus masculus; nec de facili vel passim plures admittantur . . .*"[30]

In the year 1287, a Provincial Council held at Exeter, England, repeated in its statutes the legislation of the Council of Worcester, and decreed that only three persons might act as sponsors in Baptism.[31]

In France, the Synodal Constitutions of Paris, from the thirteenth century till the time of the Council of Trent, permitted three persons, but no more than that number.[32]

The Synodal Statutes of Cambrai, however, in the thirteenth century, permitted that two male sponsors and two female, officiate. Moreover, two secular priests, and two religious, might be added to this number, if the parents of the child so desired.[33]

The Synod of Tournay, held in 1481, declared that more than three could be permitted, when the sponsors were of high social rank, or in sacred orders.[34]

Despite the statutes of Synods and Councils, many sponsors in excess of the number prescribed or allowed, were employed. In Venice, the children of noblemen

28. C. VI; SS. Concilia, XI, 1112.
29. Binterim, Anton, "*Die Vorzueglichsten Denkwerdigkeiten der Christ-Katholischen Kirche,*" vol. I, p. 195.
30. Caput V; SS. Concilia, XI, 575.
31. Caput XI de Baptismo; SS. Concilia, 1267.
32. Corblet, "*Histoire du Sacrement de Bapteme,*" lib XII, cap 7.
33. Martene, "*Vetera Monumenta,*" tom VII, col. 1293.
34. Schunnat, "*Concilia Germanica,*" tom V, col. 535.

had as many as twenty sponsors, and sometimes even more, although only one of them was permitted to hold the child over the font.[35]

In Germany, the number of sponsors was also multiplied, in order to assure to the child more protectors, and likewise to procure for it a larger number of gifts from the different godparents.[36]

In certain parts of France and Switzerland, a society composed of numerous individuals, such as a town or village, or a corporation of merchants, etc., was chosen as the sponsor.[37]

Out of such practice grew abuses. The consequent multiplicity in the matrimonial impediments of spiritual relationship arising from the use of numerous sponsors must have caused much confusion and complicity in relationship. Such a condition of affairs would naturally disturb the public ecclesiastical matrimonial discipline. The Council of Trent, wishing to remedy this condition, decreed that there should be only one sponsor at Baptism, or at most, two. "*Docet experientia, propter multitudinem prohibitionum, multoties in casibus prohibitis ignoranter contrahi matrimonia, in quibus vel non sine magno peccato perseveratur, vel ea non sine magno scandalo dirimuntur. Volens itaque sancta synodus huic incommodo providere, et a cognationis spiritualis impedimento incipiens statuit ut unus tantum, sive vir sive mulier, juxta sacrorum instituta canonum, vel ad summum unus et una baptizatum de baptismo suscipiant . . .*"[38]

This legislation of the Council of Trent became effective for the universal Church, and has remained unchanged from that time till the present. It is repeated in the Code by canon 764—"*Patrinus unus tantum, licet*

35. Corblet, "*Histoire du Sacrement de Bapteme,*" lib XII, cap 7.
36. Corblet, ibid.
37. Corblet, ibid.
38. Sessio XXIV, de refor. matr., cap II; SS. Concilia, XIV, 877.

diversi sexus a baptizando, vel ad summum unus et una adhibeantur."

Although the Code prescribes that there should be only one sponsor, even though he be of different sex from the one to be baptized; or at most, two sponsors, one male and one female, this prescription does not bind under pain of nullity, for only those laws are to be considered as nullifying which state in express or equivalent terms that either the act is null and void, or that a certain person, or persons, is incapable of validly performing a specified act.[38a] Hence, if more than two persons, or even two of the same sex, endowed with all the qualities necessary for validly acting as sponsor, and designated by whosoever has this power, would officiate as sponsor, they would validly function and contract all the obligations and relations annexed to the office of sponsorship, and also be bound by the matrimonial impediment of spiritual relationship.[39]

The right and obligation of designating a baptismal sponsor, when the candidate for the sacrament is an adult, is primarily resident in that adult person. But when the candidate for Baptism is an infant, this right and obligation belong to the parents of the child, or those who hold the place of the parents towards the child. If those on whom this right and obligation are primarily incumbent should neglect it, this right and duty devolve upon the pastor or Ordinary of the candidate, or on the minister of the sacrament.[40]

38a. Canons 764, 11.

39. Cappello, "*De Sacramentis,*" III, 562; Vlaming, "*Praelectiones Iuris Matrim.,*" I, 379.

40. Wernz, "*Jus Decretalium,*" tom IV, n. 491, footnote 57.

CHAPTER V

Historical Development of the Qualifications for Sponsors

The reason for the existence of baptismal sponsors was to afford the person baptized with an instructor and guardian of his spiritual welfare. Saint Thomas Aquinas explains the reasons for this office, when he says, "*Quod spiritualis regeneratio, quae fit per baptismum assimilatur quodammodo generationi carnali; unde dictur* 1. *Petri,* 2; '*Sicut modo geniti infantes, rationabiles, sine dolo, lac concupiscite.' In generatione carnali parvulus nuper natus indiget nutrice, et paedogogo; unde et in spirituali generatione baptismi requiritur aliquis, qui fungatur vice nutricis, et paedagogi, informando, et instruendo eum, quasi novitium in fide, de his quae pertinent ad fidem, et vitam christianam; ad quod praelati Ecclesiae vacare non possunt, circa communem curam populi occupati; parvuli enim et novitii indigent speciali cura praeter communem; et ideo requiritur, quod aliquis suscipiat baptizatum de sacro fonte, quasi in suam instructionem, et tutelam.*"[1]

If the parents of the child were of true Christian faith, the duty of religious education of the child was primarily incumbent upon them; but if they were incapable of, or negligent in this obligation, it then devolved upon the sponsor to fulfill it.[2] Hence, there were certain qualifications demanded of one who would presume to accept this office. Moreover, since it was a sacred function, it was not sufficient that the sponsors

1. S. Thom., "*Summa Theol.,*" III, q. 67.
2. S. Thom., "*Summa Theol.,*" III, q. 67, art. 8.

chosen be acceptable to the parents of the child to be baptized; or to an adult candidate who had chosen them, but it was necessary that they fulfill certain conditions required by ecclesiastical law.

Catechumens, heretics and public sinners, that is, persons who were never in full communion with the Church, since they were never baptized; or else, such as had forfeited the privileges of their Baptism, by their errors or crimes, were not permitted to act an sponsors.[3] This restriction is implicitly contained in a letter of St. Augustine in which he tells a Bishop Boniface not to be alarmed concerning the validity of the Baptism of children who are presented by unworthy sponsors; or rather, by a sponsor who does not make the proper intention for the child who is incapable of so doing. In such an event, says St. Augustine, the Church supplies the necessary intention for the child.

The words of St. Augustine in treating this manner are as follows: *"Nec illud te moveat, quod quidem non ea fide ad Baptismum percipiendum parvulos ferunt, ut gratia spirituali ad vitam regenerentur aeternam, sed quod eos putant hoc remedio temporalem retinere vel recipere sanitatem. Non enim propterea illi non regenerantur, quia non ab istis hac intentione offeruntur. Celebrantur enim per eos necessaria ministeria, et verba sacramentorum, sine quibus consecrari parvulus non potest. Spiritus autem ille sanctus qui habitat in sanctis, . . . agit quod agit etiam per servitutem, aliquando non solum simpliciter ignorantium verum etiam damnabiliter indignorum. Offeruntur quippe parvuli ad percipiendam spiritualem gratiam, non tam ab eis quorum gestantur manibus (quamvis et ab ipsis, si et boni fideles sunt), quam ab universa societate sanctorum atque fidelium. Ab omnibus namque offerri recte intel-*

3. Bingham, "*Antiquities of the Christian Church,*" lib XI, cap 8, sect. X.

ligentur, quibus placet quod offeruntur, et quorum sancta atque individua charitate ad communicationem, Sancti Spiritus adjuvantur. Tota hoc ergo mater Ecclesia, quae in sanctis est, facit, quia tota omnes, tota singulos parit."[4] The clause, "*si et ipsi boni fideles sunt,*" would imply that only those who satisfy the conditional qualifications of being among the *bonos fideles* were considered as capable and acceptable persons to function as sponsors.

Moreover, those who were not in communion with the Church could not perform the customary solemn baptismal ceremony of ancient times, when the sponsor received Holy Communion with the newly baptized every day during the octave following the Baptism.[5]

In the ancient Church the usual and most common practice of conferring Baptism was by immersion.[6] The ancient Christians thought that immersion, or burying under water, represented more forcibly the death, burial and resurrection of Christ, as well as our own death unto sin.[7] That persons to be baptized were divested of all clothing, and entered the sacred font naked, is evident from the writings of the Fathers. St. Chrysostom, speaking of Baptism, says that men were as naked as Adam in Paradise, but with this difference: Adam was naked because he had sinned, but in Baptism, a man was naked that he might be freed from sin.[8]

St. Ambrose says that the men came as naked to the font, as they came into the world—"*Nudi in saeculo nascimur, nudi etiam accedimus ad lavacrum.*"[9] Saint Cyril of Jerusalem makes note of this custom, and gives reasons for it in an instruction to some persons newly

4. St. Augustine, "*Epist. ad Bonifacium,*" MPL, XXXIII, 361-362.
5. Martene, "*De Antiquis Ritibus,*" I, cap I, art. XVI, n. XI.
6. Martene, "*De Antiquis Ritibus,*" I, cap I, art. XIV, n. V.
7. Bingham, "*Antiquities of the Christian Church,*" lib XI, cap 11, sec. I.
8. St. Chrysostom, "*Homilia VI in Coloss.,*" MPG, LXII, 542.
9. St. Ambrose, "*Serm. XX,*" MPL, XVII, 642.

baptized: "As soon as you came into the inner part of the baptistery, you put off your clothes, which is an emblem of putting off the *old man* with his deeds; and being thus divested, you stood naked, imitating Christ, who was naked upon the Cross . . . O, wonderful thing! you were naked in the sight of men, and were not ashamed, in this truly imitating the first man Adam, who was naked in Paradise, and was not ashamed."[10]

That this was the general practice, may be ascertained from a letter of St. Chrysostom. There was no exception made with the Baptism of women or infants, unless sickness or disability made it necessary to vary from the usual form. Saint Chrysostom, in describing the barbarous proceedings of his enemies against him, tells that they came armed into the Church, on the Saturday before Easter, and by violence expelled the clergy, and killed many. This scandalous conduct so terrified the catechumens who were in the baptistery at the time, and who were divested in order to be baptized, that they fled away naked.[11]

Since the general practice of the early Church was to administer Baptism by immersion, the dictates of Christian modesty, especially in the case of adults, required that the sponsor be of the same sex as the person to be baptized. The sponsor assisted the neophyte emerging from the saving waters and clothed him in the ceremonial white garment.[12] Hence, the Apostolic Constitutions decreed that deacons should perform this office for men, and deaconesses for women, "*Ac virum quidem suscipiat diaconus, mulierem vero diaconissa, ut honeste et a quibus decet, fiat signum infractum.*"[13]

Later, when in most cases the candidates for Bap-

10. St. Cyril of Jerusalem, "*Catech. Myst.,*" n. XX, MPG, XXXIII, 1078.
11. St. Chrysostom, "*Epist. I ad Innocentem,*" MPG, LII, 533.
12. Bingham, "*Antiquities of the Christian Church,*" lib XII, cap IV, sect. 1-4, notes 1-12.
13. Apost. Const., lib III, cap 16; cf. Ss. Concilia, tom I, col. 321.

tism were infants, and the practice of Baptism by infusion became more or less general, the reason for this precept practically ceased to exist, so that the law of having a sponsor of the same sex was not as strictly insisted upon.

When the candidate for Baptism was able to make the profession of faith, and to reply for himself to the questions proposed by the minister of the sacrament, the sponsor was not allowed to answer for him. As Saint Augustine observes, "*Cum pro parvulis alii respondent, ut inpleatur erga eos celebratio sacramenti, valet utique ad eorum consecrationem, quia ipsi pro se respondere non possunt. At si pro eo, qui respondere potest, alius respondeat, non itidem valet. Ex qua regula evangelii dictum est quod omnes eum leguntur, naturaliter movet, 'Aetatem habet; pro ipse se loquatur.'*"[14] From this passage in Saint Augustine, it may be inferred that the sponsor who would make the baptismal promises for another unable to do so, must be of sufficient age and intelligence, as to have his testimony acceptable according to the requisites of ecclesiastical law.

Since it was obligatory upon the sponsor to see to the religious and moral well-being of his charge, both before and after the Baptism, certain other positive qualifications were demanded of him. The fourth Council of Carthage decreed that women who were to instruct and sponsor the illiterate and unlearned women preparing for Baptism should be of sufficient learning as to be able to teach their pupils, how to answer the interrogations which the minister should propose in conferring the sacrament, and how to order their mode of living, and direct their conduct in the way of Christian virtue, after they had received Baptism, "*Viduae vel sanctaemoniales quae ad ministerium baptizandarum mulierum eliguntur,*

14. St. Augustine, "*De Baptismo,*" lib IV, c. 24; cf. c. 77, D. IV, de cons.

tam instructi sint ad officium ut possint apto et sancto sermone docere imperitas et rusticas mulieres, tempore quo baptizandae sunt, qualiter baptizatori respondeant, et qualiter accepto baptismate vivant."[15]

The Council of Calchuthensis, held in the year 787, required that the sponsors be sufficiently instructed in order to teach the Lord's Prayer and the Creed to their godchildren. The prescriptions of the Council read, "*Secundo capitulo docuimus, ut baptismus secundum canonica statuta exerceatur, et non alio tempore nisi pro magna necessitate; et ut omnes generaliter Symbolum et orationem dominicam sciant; et illi qui parvolus de sacro fonte suscipiunt, et pro non loquentibus respondent, ob renuntiationem satanae, et operum et pomparum ejus, sciant se fideijussores ipsorum esse dominum pro ipsa sponsione; ut dum ad perfectionem aetatis pervenerint, doceant eos praedictam orationem dominican et Symbolum, quia nisi fecerint districte ab eis exigetur, quod pro non loquentibus Deo promittitur. Ideo generaliter omni vulgo praecipimus hoc memoriae mandari.*"[16]

That the practice of parents acting as sponsors for their own children was quite common in the time of Saint Augustine, we know from a letter he wrote to Bishop Boniface concerning this matter. Boniface, it seems, was of the opinion that only the parents could perform this sacred function, for he had written to Augustine, "*Ut sicut parentes fuerunt auctores ad eorum poenam, per fidem parentum identidem justificentur.*"[17] Saint Augustine, wishing to correct this false opinion of Boniface, answered, "*Illud autem nolo te fallat, ut existimes reatus vinculum ex Adam tractum, aliter non posse disrumpi, nisi parvuli ad percipiendam Christi gratiam a parentibus offerantur . . . cum videas multos*

15. Concil. Carthag. IV, c. 12; cf. Harduin, "*Acta Concil.*," I, 979.
16. Ss. Concilia, VI, 1863.
17. St. Augustine, "*Epist. ad Bonifacium*," MPL, XXXIII, 362.

non offeri a parentibus, sed etiam a quibuslibet extraneis, sicut a dominis servuli aliquando offerentur. Et nonnunquam mortuis parentibus suis parvuli baptizantur, ab eis oblati qui illis hujusmodi misericordiam praebere potuerunt. Aliquando etiam quos crudeliter parentes exposuerunt nutriendos a quibuslibet, nonnunquam a sacris virginibus colliguntur, et ab eis offeruntur ad Baptismum; quae certe proprios filios nec habuerunt ullos, nec habere disponunt."[18] Although Saint Augustine denies that the parents of a child must be its sponsors, and cites many instances in which persons other than the parents officiated, still, the examples he alleges are somewhat extraordinary, and there seems to be the insinuation that ordinarily parents functioned as sponsors for their children.

There is probably no explicit prohibition to parents functioning as sponsors for their offspring, before the early part of the ninth century. The Council of Munich held in the year 813, forbade parents to act in this capacity. The fifty-fifth canon of the Council reads, "*Nullus igitur proprium filium vel filiam de fonte baptismatis suscipiat.*"[19]

The sixth Council of Arles, held in the same year of 813, in emphasizing and demanding that children should receive the proper religious instruction, clearly distinguishes between the incumbents of this obligation, namely, the parents and the sponsors. From this it might be inferred that the general practice of parents acting as sponsors had considerably decreased. The Council admonishes, "*Ut parentes filios suos et patrini eos, quos de sacro fonte lavacri suscipiunt, erudire summopere studeant, illi quia eos genuerunt, et eis a Domino dati sunt; isti quia pro eis fideijussores existunt.*"[20]

---

18. St. Augustine, "*Epist. ad Bonifacium,*" MPL, XXXIII, 362.
19. Ss. Concilia, VII, 1252.
20. Canon XIX; Cf. Ss. Concilia, VII, 1238.

In the year 829, the sixth Council of Paris explicitly excluded those who were unbaptized, or insufficiently instructed in the rudiments of the Faith, from officiating as sponsors. The seventh chapter of this Council's statutes reads, "*Quia illi qui in sponsione aliquos de sacrosancto fonte suscipiunt, nec fidei, nec baptismatis sacramento sunt instructi, et idcirco eos quos suscipiunt et secundum sanctorum patrum documenta docere debuerant, erudire nequeunt. Qualiter autem hi de sacro fonte alios suscipiunt instruere debeant, beatus Augustinus in sermone habito ad populum demonstrat dicens; 'Quicumque igitur viri, quaecumque mulieres de sacro fonte filios spiritualiter susceperunt, cognoscant se pro eis fideijussores extitisse apud Deum,' et ideo necesse est, ut castigent, atque corripiant ut castitatem custodiant, virginitatem usque ad nuptias servent, et ceteris bonis operibus dediti sunt.*"[21] The thirty-fourth canon of this same Council of Paris forbids public sinners, and those under ban of excommunication to act as baptismal sponsor, "*Illos tamen specialiter ab his officiis removendos judicamus, ne alios de sacrosancto fonte baptismatis suscipiant, . . . qui et communione canonica privati, et poenitentiae publicae sunt subacti.*"[22]

In the "*Capitularia Regum Francorum,*" those who have forfeited their good reputation by sin or crime, are declared ineligible to act as sponsor, "*Qui et communione canonica privati et publicae poenitentiae sunt subacti, donec per poenitentiam satisfactionis reconciliationem mereantur, vel etiam illi qui tale peccatum commissum habent, pro quo publica poentitentia plectendi et ligandi sunt.*"[23]

The Council of Metz, held in the year 888, demanded that only those who professed the Catholic Faith be

21. Ss. Concilia, VII, 1603.
22. Ss. Concilia, VII, 1607.
23. Martene, "*De Antiquis Ritibus,*" I, cap I, art. XVI, n. XIII.

admitted as sponsors. The sixth canon of this Council reads, "*Et nullus alteri suscipiat a fonte infantem, nisi qui apprime signaculum, id est, abrenuntiationem diaboli, et professionem fidei catholicae, tenuerit.*"[24]

It was not before the sixth century that religious were forbidden to function as sponsors. The Council of Auxerre, held in the year 578, decreed, "*Nec licet Abbati, vel monacho, de Baptismo suscipere filios, nec commatres habere.*"[25] This restriction was repeated by Pope Gregory the Great. In a letter written about the year 584, to one Valentinus, an abbot, he says, "*Pervenit ad nos quod in monasterio tuo passim mulieres ascendant, et quod est gravius, monachos tuos sibi commatres facere, et ex hoc incautam cum eis communionem habere. Ne ergo hac occasione humani generis inimicus sua eos (quod absit) calliditate decipiat, ideo hujus te percepti serie conmonemus, ut neque mulieres in monasterio tuo deinceps qualibet occasione permittas ascendere, neque monachos tuos sibi conmatres facere.*"[26] In the Capitularia Monachorum, of the year 817, is found, "*Monachi sibi conpatres conmatresve non faciant.*"[27]

The Roman Ritual authorized by Pope Paul V, on 17 June, 1614, concisely sums up the qualifications required by the earlier Councils and Synods of one who would function as baptismal sponsor. In the section, "*De patrinis,*" the Roman Ritual prescribes, "*Parochus antequam ad baptizandum accedat, ab iis ad quos spectat, exquirat diligenter, quem vel quos Susceptores seu Patrinos eligerint, qui infantem de sacro fonte, suscipiant, ne plures quam licet, aut indignos aut ineptos admittat. . . . non admittantur . . . baptizandi pater aut mater. Hos autem Patrinos saltem in aetate pubertatis, ac Sacramento Confirmationis consignatos esse, maxime*

24. Ss. Concilia, IX, 414.
25. c. 103, D. IV, de cons.
26. c. 20, c. XVIII, q. 2.
27. Lib. VII, n. 484; cf. c. 104, D. IV, de cons.

convenit. Sciant praeterea Parochi, ad hoc munus non esse admittendos infideles, aut hacreticos, non publice excommunicatos, aut interdictos, non publice criminosos, aut infames, nec praeterea qui sana mente non sunt, neque qui ignorant rudimenta fidei. Haec enim Patrini spirituales filios suos, quos de Baptismate fonte susceperint, ubi opus fuerit, opportune docere tenentur. Praeterea ad hoc etiam admitti non debent Monachi, vel Sanctimoniales, neque alii cujusvis Ordinis Regulares a saeculo segregati.[28]

The "*Catechismus Concilii Tridentini,*" published by order of Pope Pius V, provides, "*Quivis promiscue ad susceptoris munere non est admittendus . . . cuinam hominum generi sanctae hujus tutulae administratio non sit, nimirum eis, qui eam genere aut fideliter nolint, aut sedulo, et accurate non queant. Quo circa praeter naturales parentes quibus non licet eam curationem suscipere . . . haeretici in primis, Judaei, Infideles, ab hoc munere omnino prohibendi sunt, ut qui in ea cogitatione et semper cura versentur, ut fidei veritatem mendaciis semper obscurent, atque omnem Christianam pietatem evertant.*"[29]

The "*Rituale Sacramentorum ad usum Ecclesia Mediolanensis,*" published at Milan in 1613, during the episcopacy of Saint Charles Borromeo, excludes the secular clergy who are in major orders from acting as sponsors. This is probably the first prohibition to the secular clergy acting in this capacity. Prior legislation excluded only the Regulars. Moreover, lay people who lived at a considerable distance, which would interfere with the performance of their duties towards their godchildren, and visitors or strangers, who were not sufficiently known in the locality, were not allowed to officiate as baptismal sponsors.

---

28. Rituale Romanum, tit II, cap 1, nn. 22-26, "*De Sacr. Bapt.*"
29. Catechismus Concil. Trident., §II, "*De Sacr. Bapt.,*" n. 29.

Under the title, "*De caeremoniis, quae peracto Baptismo servantur,*" the Milan Ritual reads, "*Ex antiquissima Catholicae Ecclesiae consuetudine, cum praeter ministrum, qui Baptismum conficit, alii etiam ad sacram ablutionem adhibeantur, qui patrini, aut compatres vocantur, Parochus, de eis ut infra animadvertat ac servabit. Non adhiberi sinet ex eis plures, quam unum tantum, sive virum, sive mulierem, ex sacrorum canonum praescripto, vel ad summum unum et unam, ut a Concilio Tridentino statutum, est, non tamen simul virum et uxorem adhibebit. Ne excommunicatos, interdictos, publice criminosos, infamesque, pueros natu minores quatuordecim annis; nec praeterea, qui sana mente non sunt: neque eos, qui in Pascha communionem non sumpserint; nec vero Monachos, Regulares, clericosque saeculares sacris initatios, ad infantem de Baptismo clericosque saeculares sacris initiatos, ad infantem de Baptismo suscipiendum adhiberi sinet. Nec praeterea illos, quos putet ignorare Symbolum, orationemque Dominicam, salutationem Angelicam, rudimentaque fidei Christianae; neque item eos, qui nondum Confirmationis Sacramentum susceperint . . . Eam quoque rationem cohortando habebit, ut ne peregrini, hospites, ignoti, et ii deinque compatres adhibeantur, quorum domicilium longe absit, veresimile non est, consuetudinem inter baptizatum, eosque ita futuram, ut suscepti muneris functionem in eo instruendo praestare possint. Praemonebit autem accurate parentes paulo ante Baptismi administrationem, ut compatres tales deligant, quales eos esse oportet, qui et vitae exemplis, et Christiana disciplina, castisque moribus alios instruere debent.*"[30]

The qualifications prescribed for baptismal sponsors have practically remained unchanged since the beginning of the eighteenth century. Instructions and rescripts from the Holy See, and enactments of Provin-

30. Trombelli, "*Tractatus de Sacramentis,*" tom II, diss. VI, n. 11.

cial Councils and Synods, have checked any derogations from the requirements of the common law, which contrary custom may have sought to introduce. Many reasons, from various countries and at different times, have been presented to the Holy See, seeking, as it were, a mitigation of the law excluding heretics from the office of sponsor, but the Holy See has conceded no dispensations on this point.

The Congregation of the Holy Office, on October 14, 1676, in reply to inquiries from Bosnia, strictly forbade the admission of heretics as sponsors, even though the strongest reasons of friendship and familiarity prompted the choice of such a person.[31] A later instruction to the missionaries in Egypt, drawn up in accordance with the order of Benedict XIV, and published by the Holy Office on 9 December, 1745, reiterates the prohibition of infidels and heretics officiating at Catholic Baptism as sponsors. Only the danger to life itself, would excuse from blame any priest who admitted such to this sacred function.[32] In January, 1763, an instruction of the Holy Office to the Prefect of the Missions in Tripoli, repeated that non-Catholics could not be admitted to the office of sponsor, but for good reasons might be permitted to attend the ceremony as a witness, but not by any means as sponsor.[33] Two decisions of the Holy Office, under the dates, 30 June, and 7th July, 1864, again declared heretics and schismatics ineligible as baptismal sponsors, even though they would perform this function through a Catholic proxy.[34] An instruction sent to the missionaries in India on 8 September, 1869, calls the practice of admitting heretics as sponsors a serious abuse.[35]

---

31. Collectanea, S. C. Prop. Fide, n. 211.
32. Collectanea, S. C. Prop. Fide, n. 355.
33. Collectanea, S. C. Prop. Fide, n. 447.
34. Collectanea, S. C. Prop. Fide, n. 1257.
35. Collectanea, S. C. Prop. Fide, n. 1346.

When there was no eligible candidate available to choose as sponsor, it was permitted that the parents supply the functions of sponsor at the solemn ceremony of Baptism, but they were not to be considered as the formal sponsors of the child, and that in such a case no spiritual relationship was contracted. In accordance with this same response of the Holy Office, 15 September, 1869, the parents were allowed to act as proxies for an acceptable sponsor if he could not be present at the time of the ceremony.[36]

A certain pastor in Hungary cited an instance where a mother had apostatized, because a heretic whom she had selected as sponsor for her child had been rejected by the pastor. The Holy Office was asked whether, under such circumstances, it would be licit to permit a non-Catholic to function. The answer given on 3 May, 1893, was in the negative, and it was added that in such a case when no acceptable sponsor could be procured, the solemn ceremony could be performed without a sponsor.[37]

The Sacred Congregation of Rites, on 23 August, 1713, declared that the local Ordinary, according to his prudent judgment, could dispense children under twelve or fourteen years, which was the age generally required by the Roman and other rituals to act as baptismal sponsor.[38]

The new legislation of the Code makes practically no changes in the qualifications demanded of those who would officiate as baptismal sponsors. They are the same as those required by the common law of the Church prior to the Code. There is, however, a distinction made in the new legislation which divides these requisites

36. Collectanea, S. C. Prop. Fide, n. 1247.
37. Collectanea, S. C. Prop. Fide, n. 1813.
38. Collectanea, S. C. Prop. Fide, n. 284.

into two distinct classes. There are those qualifications necessary that one can validly be a sponsor; and others, that one may licitly function in that capacity.

The conditions demanded by the Code that one can be a sponsor at Baptism, are enumerated in canon 765, and are treated in Chapter seven.

CHAPTER VI

SPIRITUAL RELATIONSHIP AND DOUBTFUL BAPTISM

Baptism, like all the Sacraments, depends for its validity upon the placing of certain essential conditions of divine institution. The principal elements determining the validity of this sacrament are the matter, form and intention of the minister. A substantial defect in any of these three elements would render the sacrament invalid. A well founded, prudent doubt whether the conditions for validity have actually been fulfilled renders the Baptism doubtful.

The necessity of sacramental Baptism for the individual as a means of salvation arises from the supreme will of Christ: "Amen, Amen, I say to you, unless a man be born again of water and the Holy Ghost, he cannot enter into the kingdom of God."[1] The foundation of this necessity is based on the defiled state of the children of Adam and the supernatural quality of the glory of heaven. The child of Adam must be made a child of God by the regenerating influence of the Divine Spirit, and until it take place, entrance into the Church of God on earth, and into the glorious kingdom of God above, is impossible.

Since the sacrament of Baptism imprints an indelible spiritual character on the soul of its recipient, it cannot be repeated on the same subject.[2] So enormous, and so vitally important to the individual are the effects that follow from Baptism, it is of no little moment that the sacrament should have been validly administered.

1. John, III, 5.
2. Canon 732, §1.

Therefore, the Church has wisely provided that if there be any prudent doubt concerning the validity or existence of a prior Baptism, the sacrament should be conferred again conditionally.[2a]

The conditional repetition of Baptism is an extraordinary case, entailing two ceremonies. This gives rise to an inquiry concerning the mutual relations and obligations incurred by the sponsors and their godchildren in each of the three possible cases. It may be that the same sponsor functions at both ceremonies, or different sponsors may have acted at each Baptism; or there may have been a sponsor at only one of the Baptisms. The answer to this inquiry is contained in the prescriptions of canon 763, to a consideration of which we now proceed.

When Baptism is administered again conditionally the same sponsor who formerly officiated in that capacity should be employed in as far as it is possible to have him; except in this given case, a sponsor is not necessary in a conditional Baptism, and the precept to have a sponsor ceases to obtain. "*Cum baptismus iteratus sub conditione, idem patrinus, quatenus fieri possit, adhibeatur, qui in priore baptismo forte adfuit; extra hunc casum in baptismo conditionato patrinus non est necessarius.*"[3]

The clause, "*quatenus fieri possit,*" allows a reasonable and serious cause to excuse from this precept. Hence, a grave inconvenience for the sponsor of the former Baptism to attend, such as his removal to a great distance, sickness, etc., would excuse. The former sponsor, however, could function through the medium of proxy. There may be, however, impediments of law which may have intervened in the meantime to prohibit such a one from acting as sponsor, such as the loss of

2a. Canon 732, §2.
3. Canon 763, §1.

the use of reason, unwillingness or retraction of intention to assume this office, heresy or schism, ecclesiastical penalty, etc. If he lacked any of the essential qualifications demanded by canon 765, he cannot, of course, validly function in the capacity of sponsor. If any of the prohibitions of canon 766 impede him for licitly acting as sponsor, he cannot licitly act except by ecclesiastical dispensation.

When baptism is repeated conditionally, neither the sponsor who functioned in the prior Baptism, nor the sponsor who officiated at the latter ceremony, contracts the spiritual relationship, unless he be the one and the same person who functioned as sponsor at both ceremonies. This special disposition and exemption of the legislator is contained in canon 763, §2, *"Iterato baptismo sub conditione, neque patrinus qui priori baptismo adfuit, neque qui posteriori, cognationem spiritualem contrahit, nisi idem patrinus in utroque baptismo adhibitus fuerit."*

It will be noted this paragraph speaks of a repeated conditional Baptism, and not simply of a conditional Baptism. Hence, one who would act as sponsor at a conditional Baptism could not be said to be exempt from the impediments of spiritual relationship by reason of this canon. The fundamental basis of the spiritual relationship as a matrimonial impediment is true, valid, sacramental Baptism.[4] When a condition is placed in the administration of Baptism so that the verification or realization of that condition will determine the validity, or invalidity of the Sacrament, the consequent existence or non-existence of the impediment of spiritual relationship resulting from that administration of Baptism, will be proportionately contingent on the Sacrament's validity. If the validity of the Sacrament is doubtful, the consequent spiritual relationship is equally

4. Canons 768 and 1079.

doubtful. But this does not mean that the impediment does not bind, because of this doubt. If the doubt can be resolved so that the validity or nullity of the Baptism can be ascertained, then the spiritual relationship begotten by the sacrament can be judged existent or non-existent. If, however, it is not possible to resolve the doubt concerning the validity of the Baptism, the existence of any spiritual relationship would constitute a doubtful impediment *dubio facti,* from which the Ordinary can dispense.[5]

Hence, in practice, if this condition should arise, namely, when a doubt of fact exists concerning the impediment of spiritual relationship by reason of a doubtful Baptism, a dispensation should be petitioned before the marriage is contracted. If the doubt should arise after the marriage is contracted, the validity of the marriage is to be presumed till the contrary is proved.[6]

The opinions of canonists who wrote before the Code, seem to offer a variety of conclusions regarding the force of the impediment arising from a doubtfully valid Baptism. Gasparri writes, "*In dubio de validitate Baptismi* (*aut confirmationis*), *cum in utraque parte adest probabilitas, etiam cognatio, et consequenter impedimentum dubium est, ideoque nullum, Exinde patet quid dicendum in casu baptismatis denuo collati sub conditione. Si dubium de priori baptismo est negativum, idest pro illius valore nulla adest solida positiva ratio, cognatio et impedimentum oritur ex secundo, non ex primo; et si deinde constet primum baptismum fuisse validum, jam oritur ex primo, non ex secundo. Si dubium est positivum, idest pro utraque parte adsunt probabiles rationes; ex neutro oritur, nisi utrique baptismati eaedem personae operam navaverint; et si deinde certa*

5. Canon 15.
6. Canon 1014.

evadat unius validitas, ex eo oritur, non ex alio; sed matrimonio jam forte contracto jam non nocet, quia impedimentum dubium, impedimentum nullum."[7]

It would seem that the conclusion of the eminent canonist, "*impedimentum dubium, impedimentum nullum,*" is too broad, and should be subjected to the distinction between a doubt of fact (*dubium facti*) and a doubt of law (*dubium iuris*). If an impediment is doubtful by a doubt of law, then the conclusion, "*impedimentum dubium, impedimentum nullum,*" may be conceded; if the impediment is doubtful by a doubt of fact, it could hardly be classed as an "*impedimentum nullum.*"

However, Gasparri modifies this statement when he discusses doubtful matrimonial impediments in general, for he writes: "*Quid agendum in praxi in casu hujus dubii facti tantum. Nempe ante omnia diligens inquisitio facienda est: quisque enim ad matrimonium est admittendus, nisi impedimento prohibeatur. Post hanc inquisitionem Ordinario triplex casus occurrere potest:*

1. *Non existentia impedimenti est moraliter certa, ita ut Ordinarius dubitare prudenter nequeat. In hoc casu permittet matrimonium sine ulla dispensatione, quia illa moralis certitudo profecto sufficit in agendo, etsi, si, ea non obstante, impedimentum adsit, matrimonium, juxta plures, coram Deo viribus careat.*

2. *Existentia impedimenti probabilis est, ita ut Ordinarius prudens, omnibus perpensis, aliquod dubium habeat. In hoc casu matrimonium non permittet, sine dispensatione ad cautelam.*

3. *Tandem existentia impedimenti est moraliter certa, ita ut prudenti Ordinario nullum fundatum de*

7. "*De Matrimonio,*" I, 835.

ea dubium sit. In hoc casu petenda et obtinenda est dispensatio vel sanatio in radice, non quidem ad cautelam, sed pure et simpliciter."[8]

St. Alphonsus, considering the question of spiritual relationship arising from a doubtful Baptism, proposes the question: *"An suscipiens in Baptismo collato sub conditione contrahat cognationem? Respondendum, si de primo Baptismo adsit dubium dumtaxat negativum, omnino affirmandum cum communi, quia nulla tunc urget ratio pro valore anterioris Baptismi, et presumptio stat pro valore secundi. Secus tamen si dubium sit positivum. Et hoc satis est probabile juxta dicenda de Matrim, n.* 901, *ubi dicemus cum communi DD. bene posse contrahi matrimonium, quando post adhibitam diligentiam, nullum impedimentum certo adesse probatur."*[9] This opinion of Saint Alphonsus seems to be a forerunner of Gasparri's, namely, when there is equal probability concerning the existence or non-existence of a matrimonial impediment, one is free to contract marriage. He distinguishes, however, between an impediment *in dubio iuris,* and one *in dubio facti.* Only the former, he says, may be classed as an *impedimentum nullum.*[10]

Sanchez holds that when the existence of spiritual relationship depends on a doubtfully valid Baptism, the existence of the relationship is to be presumed till the invalidity of the Baptism is established. Treating this question, Sanchez writes, *"Et generaliter quoties baptismus vel confirmatio sunt irrita, dicendum est, ex eis nullam, oriri cognationem. Hinc deducitur ex baptismo iterato sub-conditione, eo quod de prioris baptismi veritate dubitabatur, postquam constiterit priorem fuisse validum, non oriri cognationem. At dum id non*

8. *"De Matrimonio,"* I, 264-267.
9. St. Alphonsus, *"Theologia Moralis,"* VI, 151.
10. St. Alphonsus, *"Theologia Moralis,"* VI, 901-902.

constat, praesumet Ecclesia cognationem. Quod intelligo quando est merum dubium."[11]

However, when from repeated conditional Baptisms, the spiritual relationship arising from either of them is doubtful, and there are positive, cogent arguments adduced to support the validity of either Baptism, Sanchez allows that one may choose either Baptism to be valid, and consider the spiritual relationship consequent to the repudiated Baptism as probably nonexistent. But this opinion seems hardly conformable with his claim that as long as the invalidity of a Baptism is not established, the Church presumes the existence of spiritual relationship arising from it. However, a presentation of Sanchez's argument and an analysis of it, will show that his second conclusion is in harmony with his first. He writes, *"Nam si sint variae opiniones probabiles, dicam: deducitur, oriri cognationem spiritualem dum quis nondum integre natus baptizatur, quando baptismus est validus; nec oriri postea ex baptismo sub conditione iterato in Ecclesia propter dubium valoris prioris baptismi. Sic Navarrus . . . dicit id esse verum, licet in quacumque corporis parte fiat baptismus. Quia censet quamcumque partem aqua intingi sufficere ad baptismi veritatem. Sed bene dixit Alex. de Nevo . . . hoc pendere ex ea quaestione an baptismus in quacumque corporis parte collatus sit validus. Unde existimo non ita absolute loquendum, ut loquutus est Navarrus. Sed si in ea parte conferatur baptismus, ubi est ita certum, eum esse validum; ut non sit sub conditione iterandus, contrahetur ex eo cognatio, non autem ex iteratione: si autem dubium sit inter viros doctos an in ea parte collatus sit validus, eadem dubitatio insurget utrum ex baptismo cognatio spiritualis consurgat; et si sint duae opiniones probabiles, quarum altera neget prioris baptismi valorem; altera autem*

11. Sanchez, "*De Matrimonio,*" lib VII, disp. 62, nn. 5 and 6.

affirmet, poterit tuta conscientia quispiam utram harum eligere; et tenendo baptismum non fuisse validum, dicet consequenter probabile esse ex eo non oriri cognationem, sed ex iteratione. Contrarium vero dicet, si eam opinionem amplectatur quae sustinet priorem fuisse validum. Et cum utraque opinio sit probabilis, poterit utravis illarum tuta conscientia amplecti."[12]

The author here considers an instance where Baptism has been repeated conditionally, about which there are probable opinions of reputable theologians differing concerning the validity of the sacrament: some supporting the validity of the prior Baptism; others, contending for the validity of the latter Baptism. In such a case, the author proposes that one may adhere to either opinion. Hence, if one chose to accept that the former administration of the sacrament was invalid, the spiritual relationship could be considered as probably not existing. He does not say absolutely that the relationship does not exist, but probably does not exist. The use of the word *probabile* leaves the decision on the existence of the spiritual relationship still contingent on the validity or invalidity of the Baptism, and rightly so, because although one may be inclined to doubt the validity of the former Baptism, this belief is only founded on presumption, which seems to resolve the question to the condition cited above where the existence of spiritual relationship contingent on a doubtful Baptism was presumed to obtain till the doubt was resolved.

Schmalzgrueber and Reiffenstuel do not discuss the question of spiritual relationship arising from a doubtful Baptism, but merely point out that there can be no spiritual relationship from an invalid Baptism.[13]

Wernz, dealing with question in point, writes, "*Quodsi valor baptismi vel confirmationis propter*

12. Sanchez, "*De Matrimonio,*" lib VII, disp. 62, n. 7.
13. Schmalzgrueber, "*Jus Eccl. Universum,*" §III, tit XI, n. 40. Reiffenstuel, "*Jus Canonicum Universum,*" lib IV, tit XI, n. 13.

rationes utrimque solide probabiles sit vere dubius, etiam cognatio spiritualis est dubia, quae nequit inducere certum impedimentum matrimonii. Hinc si in casu dubii positivi sacramentum baptismi vel confirmationis sub conditione iteretur, ex neutra sacramenti administratione cognatio spiritualis certo oritur, nisi eaedem personae, v. g. eidem patrini in utroque collatione intervenerint. Quodsi postea certa fiat validitas unius administrationis sacramenti, ex illa, non ex altera impedimentum matrimonii inducitur, sed certitudo superveniens certo obstat valori matrimonii antea jam contracti. Si accidat, ut dubium de valore prioris administrationis sacramenti sit mere negativum, i. e. nulla solida ratio pro valore militat, ex secunda collatione sacramenti conditionate facta, non ex prima, cognatio spiritualis cum impedimento canonico matrimonii est praesumenda. Superveniente autem certa notitia de validitate primae administrationis sacramenti, profecto ex illa, non ex secunda provenit cognatio spiritualis, sed valor matrimonii antea contracti certo negari non potest."[14]

The doctrine regarding doubtful matrimonial impediments may be briefly summarized. A matrimonial impediment may be doubtful either by a doubt of law (*dubium iuris*), or a doubt of fact (*dubium facti*). There is a doubt of fact when it is certain that an impediment would arise from a given fact, but it is doubted whether or not that fact really exists. There is a doubt of law when the existence of the fact is certain, but whether an impediment by the prescriptions of the law arises from this fact is doubtful.

If before a marriage there is a doubtful impediment by a doubt of law, and due diligence has been employed to resolve this doubt, but to no avail, then the parties are free to marry. And if, perchance, the doubt is later resolved, and the certain existence of the impediment is

14. Wernz, "*Jus Decretalium,*" tom IV, 489.

established, *e. g.*, by a declaration of the Höly See, the already contracted marriage is valid. The reasons alleged to substantiate the principle: "*impedimentum dubium, impedimentum nullum,*" were that a doubtful law did not bind (*lex dubia non obligat*), and that the Church was presumed to have supplied a dispensation in cases where there was a doubt of law. Even though at the time of the marriage the impediment might have existed, nevertheless, whilst there was a dispute among the canonists and theologians concerning its existence, and no authentic declaration of the Holy See to decide the matter, the presumption was that the Church did not urge it. The supplement of dispensation by the Church in marriages contracted with a doubtful impediment of law, was the common and universal opinion of the canonists and theologians, and this presumption was substantiated by many decisions of the Roman Rota, and Pontifical declarations.[15]

The slight difference between the old law and the present discipline regarding impediments doubtful by a doubt of law is concisely put by De Smet: "*Ante novam disciplinam Codicis, pariter matrimonium permittebant auctores in casu, recurrendo non ad cessationem legis, sed ad suppletionem Ecclesiae. Jam nunc radicalis est solutio—vi principii enuntiati in canone* 15: *'leges, etiam irritantes et inhabilitantes, in dubio iuris non urgent'—et, cum lex in dubio iuris simpliciter cesset, jam non est anxiandum de valore matrimonii in tali dubio jam contracti, si postea innotescat adfuisse reipsa impedimentum.*"[16]

When there is a doubtful impediment by a doubt of fact existing prior to a marriage, and after due investigation the doubt cannot be resolved, a dispensation

---

15. St. Alphonsus, "*Theologia Moralis,*" lib VI, 901; Gasparri, "*De Matrimonio,*" I, 262.
16. De Smet, "*De Sponsalibus et Matrimonio,*" tom II, 472.

should be sought *ad cautelam.*[17] For at the time the marriage is contracted, notwithstanding the doubt, the impediment *de facto* either does or does not exist. If it does exist, and no dispensation has been granted, the marriage is, by that very fact, invalid. This conclusion is evident, and supported by numerous decisions of the Holy See regarding such matrimonial cases submitted for adjudication.

Some theologians[18] held that the Church could be presumed to have dispensed in impediments *in dubio facti,* just as she did in impediments *in dubio iuris,* but the arguments of other theologians,[19] and the practice of the Pontifical tribunals in deciding such cases, refute their contentions.

Before the Code, in cases where reasonable arguments could be adduced on both sides to support the existence or non-existence of an impediment *in dubio facti,* and the doubt could not be resolved, some theologians (Sanchez, Cardenas, Tamburini, *et alii*) held that this condition constituted no more than a mere doubt, so that it was lawful for the parties to marry. The most that could be said for the validity of such marriages, is that it is doubtful. Other theologians (Vidal, Laymann, St. Alphonsus, *et alii*) contended that it was not permissible to use the above opinion, since it exposed the sacrament to the danger of invalidity.[20]

It was further disputed before the Code, whether or not an Ordinary could dispense from impediments *in dubio facti,* or whether he needed delegated faculties from the Holy See.[21]

---

17. Instr. S. C. S. Off., 9 Dec., 1874; Collectanea S. C. de Prop. Fide, n. 1427.
18. Tamburini, Dec. lib I, cap 3, sect. 3, n. 27; Bonacina et alii apud Croix, lib 6, §1, n. 118.
19. St. Alphonsus, "*Theologia Moralis,*" lib VI, n. 902; et apud ipsum, Cardenas, Viva, Croix, Gormaz ac Aversa.
20. St. Alphonsus, "*Theologia Moralis,*" lib VI, 902.
21. Sanchez, "*De Matrimonio,*" lib VIII, disp. VI, n. 18.

The above difficulties of the old law are now decided by the Code. In the present discipline, when there is an impediment *dubio facti,* it is not lawful to contract marriage unless a dispensation has been obtained, and if this impediment be one which the Holy See usually dispenses, the Ordinary has the power *ipso jure* to dispense from it.[22]

Whatever may be said for or against the arguments and opinions of the canonists prior to the Code, by virtue of the legislation of canon 763, 2, in a case of repeated conditional Baptism, the sponsor contracts no spiritual relationship, unless one and the same person acts as sponsor at both ceremonies. Vlaming asserts that to invoke this exemption in favor of the different sponsors, it makes no difference whether the reasons for repeating the conditional Baptism were founded on a negative doubt, for instance, whether a foundling child had been baptized or not, and so conditional Baptism was administered *ad cautelam;* or if the reasons for the conditional repetition were based on positive doubt, for example, a doubt concerning a substantial defect in the matter, form, or intention of the minister of the sacrament.[23] This assertion, however, should be tempered, and considered with due regard for canon 732, 2, which postulates the existence of a prudent doubt concerning the existence or validity of a former Baptism, before this sacrament can be conditionally readministered. Hence, if a Baptism were repeated without any prudent reason to warrant it, but rather on account of unfounded scruples, or through malice or fraud to circumvent the law, the exemptions of canon 763, 2, could not be invoked.

Furthermore, if it later be established beyond all doubt that one of these conditional administrations was certainly invalid, and the other valid, the sponsor of the

22. Canon 15; cf. De Smet, "*De Sponsalibus et Matrimonio,*" tom II, n. 472; Cappello, "*De Sacramentis,*" III, 231.
23. Vlaming, "*Praelectiones Iuris Matrimonii,*" I, 375.

valid ceremony would not thereby contract the spiritual relationship.[24] Hence, by this special disposition and exemption, no spiritual relationship is contracted by the sponsor unless the same qualified sponsor act as such on both occasions.

The Code explicitly extends this exemption to the sponsor, but what is to be said concerning the one who baptizes, or the minister of the sacrament? Does the impediment of spiritual relationship arise between the minister of a repeated conditional Baptism and the recipient of the sacrament? Some advance the opinion that since there is only explicit mention of the sponsor, the exemption from the impediment cannot be extended to the minister of the sacrament, hence the minister and the recipient of the sacrament in this case would be bound by the doubtful impediment through a doubt of fact, and if these two wished to contract marriage, unless the doubt has been resolved, they should seek a dispensation before contracting marriage.[25]

Another opinion would adduce from the apparently less stringent discipline of the Code, which seems to attempt the restriction of spiritual relationship as a matrimonial impediment, that the question of the spiritual relationship between the minister and the recipient in a repeated conditional Baptism would constitute, at most, a *dubium iuris*, which, by the prescriptions of canon 15, would be no impediment at all. In other words, this opinion extends to the minister of a repeated conditional Baptism, the same exemption granted by law to the sponsor.[26]

The arguments and conclusions advanced by Vlaming, who favors the former opinion concerning this

---

24. Cappello, "*De Sacramentis,*" III, 558; Vlaming, "*Praelectiones Iuris Matrimonii,*" I, 375.
25. De Smet, "*De Sponsalibus et Matrimonio,*" tom II, 639; Chelodi, "*Jus Matrimoniale,*" 106.
26. Cappello, "*De Sacramentis,*" III, 558.

question seem most cogent and acceptable. "*Quid vero de cognatione spirituali e baptismo conditionato baptisatum inter et baptisantem? Quum de ea Codex prorsus sileat, retinendum videtur jus praecedens hac contenttum doctrina. Si circa collationem vel valorem prioris baptismi dubium sit mere negativum, ob praesumptionem valoris tunc totam posteriori baptismo faventem, conditionate baptisans spiritualem cognationem vere contrahit. Similiter si, in hypothesi dubii veri ac postivi, conditionate rebaptizans sit ipse idem qui etiam baptismum dubie validum contulit: quia tunc plene ac certo fuit baptisato regenerationis minister et veluti pater. Extra hos casus, si nempe baptisans fuerit minister solius baptismi conditionati, ejusque collati ob dubium positivum circa baptismum anteriorem multi auctores ut olim, etiamnum inde exsurgentem dubiam cognationem ut nullam accipient. Nominatim exsurgenti inde impedimento dirimenti illud applicant; 'Impedimentum dubium, impedimentum nullum.' Huic vero doctrinae, salva reverentia erga ejus propugnatores, numquam assentire potui. Videtur enim praedicta regula hic perperam alicui casui applicari in quo nullum reapse dubium juris invenitur, sed nonnisi aliquod dubium facti. Spectato enim jure seu lege Ecclesiae, quod suppono quoad rem praesentem per Codicem non esse mutatum, etiam baptismus conditionatus, quoties regenerationem spiritualem vere et indubie infert. Quare patroni sententiae a nobis impugnatae ipsi fatentur quod, si aliquando constet de valore alterutrius baptismi, ei qui in illo operam navaverint, cognationem spiritualem inde revera contraxisse sint dicendi. Unde quaerere licet; num forte eo momento, quo e. g. de valore baptismi posterioris constare incipiat eodem cognatio spiritualis oritur? Quod profecto erit negandum; cognatio enim contrahenda non potest pendere a scientia vel dubio baptizantis, sed unice a lege Ecclesiae. Hinc, dicendum, in casu baptismi conditionati adesse merum dubium facti; seu simplicem defectum certitudinis de baptismi valore; et sic quoque merum dubium facti de cognationis existentia. In tali autem dubio e sententia jam olim longe probabiliori et nunc, e sensu contrario canonis* 15 *fere certa, opus est impedimenti dispensatione ad cautelam. Quod proinde etiam applicandum esset si ageretur de matrimonio contrahendo inter conditionate baptizantem et ab eo sic baptisatum.*[27]

27. Vlaming, "*Praelectiones Iuris Matrimonii,*" tom I, 376.

CHAPTER VII

Qualifications for Baptismal Sponsors Enumerated in the Code of Canon Law

In canons 765 and 766 the Code enumerates the qualifications demanded by the present law of those who would act in the capacity of baptismal sponsor. In canon 765 are postulated certain essential qualifications, conditions *sine qua non,* in order that one may be considered a valid sponsor. This is apparent from the wording of the Code: *"ut quis sit patrinus."* The use of the word *to be* in this connection imports either existence or non-existence; hence, unless one be endowed with these essential qualifications for acting as sponsor, his actions would be considered null and void. Furthermore, the qualifications enumerated in canon 766 are proposed before one can licitly or legally be admitted as sponsor, which implies the conditions enumerated in the preceding canon are for validity.

Baptizatus.

The first qualification demanded of a sponsor by canon 765 is that he be baptized. Juridically speaking, a person is a subject capable of rights, and duties or obligations. Canonically considered, a person is a subject capable of sustaining certain obligations, and of acquiring or obtaining certain ecclesiastical rights. Personality, or juridical capacity, is that quality by which a man becomes a person in law. This personality, or juridical capacity, in canon law, may be full and complete, or incomplete. One is considered to enjoy complete personality who is not only bound by the obligations which are enjoined by the laws of the Church, but who also enjoys all the rights granted to the status to which he belongs, whether it be lay or clerical.

One is considered as possessing incomplete personality who, though bound by all the obligations of the Church, does not enjoy all the ecclesiastical rights. Now, it is apparent that a man, by reason of his human nature, cannot have juridical personality in a supernatural society. The principle by which a man acquires juridical, canonical capacity in the supernatural society of the Church, and becomes constituted a person in it with all the rights and obligations of the Christian, is by Baptism.[1] For Baptism, as it were, is the door through which the man enters the home of the Church, and hence becomes the subject of the ecclesiastical authority and acquires the status of Christian membership. Those who have not received Baptism are not within the pale of the Church and, except indirectly, inasmuch as by her Divine foundation the Church is Catholic and seeks to effect the salvation of all, the Church does not legislate for, nor consider the unbaptized.[2] Hence, since by Baptism one is constituted a person in the Church of Christ and endowed with all the rights and dignity of a Christian, only those who have been baptized can validly function in the office of baptismal sponsor, which is an ecclesiastical office.[3]

It is of no consequence whether the baptismal rite was conferred privately or solemnly, whether, according to the Catholic Ritual, or by a non-Catholic ceremony, provided the sacrament has been validly confected. Although it is true that a non-Catholic Baptism suffices, if validly administered, it is required that the sponsor be a professed Catholic at the time he would officiate in such a capacity, as is clear from §2 of this canon.

1. canon 88.
2. canon 12.
3. canon 2256, §2.

The absurdity of having an unbaptized person act as a baptismal sponsor is obvious. The sponsor's duty is to provide for his godchild's religious education, if need be, and acquaint him of the exalted dignity and Christian heritage which Baptism confers on its recipient. Now, an unbaptized person is either ignorant of the necessity and efficacy of Baptism to the individual; or if he be cognizant of this, and still remain unbaptized, his negligence or perversity in so important a matter renders him totally unfit. Hence the Church wisely prohibits such from acting as sponsor.

Usum Rationis Assecutus.

That one can be a sponsor, he must have the use of reason, and have it *hic et nunc,* at the time of the conferring of the sacrament; he must, moreover, have the intention of accepting the office.

Regarding those who lack the use of reason, two classes may be distinguished: namely, those who habitually lack the use of reason, and those who temporarily or in a given instance, do not enjoy the use of reason. In the first class we may include children who have not yet reached the age of seven years, who are presumed to lack the use of reason.[4] This is a presumption *iuris simpliciter,*[5] and hence admits of direct or indirect proof to the contrary. So, if it can be proved that a child under seven enjoys the use of reason, he may validly function, though not licitly,[6] as sponsor.

Those who are perpetually insane, that is, those who suffer a constant, radical impotence in the exercise of the use of reason; imbeciles, whose rational faculties are so undeveloped that they may be likened to children under the age of seven years, may be ascribed to this first class. The same thing may be said of those who

4. canon 88, §3.
5. Noval, "*De Judiciis,*" §I, 561; cf. canons 1825, §2 and 1826.
6. canon 766, §1.

have been deaf, dumb and blind since their birth, who consequently have had no opportunity of developing the intellectual faculties, wherefore they may also be compared to children under seven years of age.

Under the second class we may include those who are subject to temporary spells of insanity; monomaniacs, whose mental attitude toward certain ideas is considered irrational; those suffering from total, or partial loss of memory, so as to be incapable of placing a human act; those whose rational faculties are temporarily suspended, such as those under the influence of intoxicating drink to such an extent that they can be said to be unable of performing a human act; finally, those under hypnotic influence.

The propriety of excluding those bereft of intelligence from acting as baptismal sponsors is sufficiently apparent. They are not capable of assuming any obligations, for the will is the seat of moral obligation, and those who lack the use of reason, can not place an act of consent, or an intention to accept this office, and acts that presuppose intelligence or intention in the agent are null and void when placed by persons lacking the use of reason.

Intentio munus gerendi.

It is further required that the sponsor have the intention of officiating in the capacity of sponsor. Common sense dictates that one who assumes an obligation should be cognizant of the burdens which the acceptance of such obligation entails. This accordingly presupposes a knowledge of the action which he is to perform, and the series of consequent obligations which necessarily result. Hence, one who is to function as baptismal sponsor is required to know the nature of sponsorship, and the acceptance of this incumbency must be deliberate.

The sponsor must stand in a quasi-paternal relationship to the child. On him devolves the obligation, if those obliged by nature should fail, to rear his spiritual son in Catholicism. A truly tremendous obligation, and consequently, when accepted, it is imperative that he know the person about whom this obligation revolves. As a consequence, any substantial error in regard to the person for whom he assumes this gratuitous obligation, nullifies the act. The intention of acting as an honorary witness is insufficient.[7] On the other hand, it is not necessary that the sponsor have the intention of contracting spiritual relationship, because this matrimonial impediment necessarily arises from the disposition of the Church's law.[8] It is not required that the sponsor's intention be an actual one, that is, an intention actually elicited at the time of the Baptism. Neither is a virtual intention necessary, that is, one elicited prior to the Baptism, which flows into the act but is not adverted to at the precise moment when the Baptism was performed. It is quite sufficient that the sponsor have an habitual intention, that is, an intention once elicited and never recalled, even though it is neither adverted to, nor flows into the action at the time of the Baptism.

Canon 765, §2. *"Ut quis sit patrinus, oportet;*

Ad nullam pertineat haereticam aut schismatican sectam, nec sententia condemnatoria vel declaratoria sit excommunicatus aut infamis infamia iuris aut exclusis ab actibus legitimis, nec sit clericus depositus vel degradatus."

Those belonging to heretical or schismatical sects; those who by a declaratory or condemnatory sentence are excommunicated, or infamous by law, or excluded from legal acts, or a deposed or a degraded cleric, can not be sponsors.

---

7. Wernz, "*Jus Decretalium,*" IV, 492.
8. De Smet, "*De Sponsalibus et Matrimonio,*" tom II, 639, 2.

Pertineat.

Regarding those who are members of heretical or schismatical sects, the word *pertineat* comprehends not only those who have formally affiliated themselves with such sects by having their names inscribed on their rosters, or formal profession in such sects, but also those who, by their frequent participation in the practices of these sects, manifest an adherence to them.[9]

HAERETICAM VEL SCHISMATICAM SECTAM.

According to its general signification, heresy may be objective or subjective. Objective heresy is that teaching or belief contrary to revealed truth which is falsely asserted or believed by the heretic; subjective heresy is the act by which a heretic adheres to the objective heresy. Heresy may be further distinguished into material heresy and formal heresy. Material heresy is the assent alone given by the intellect to the objective heresy but without any obstinacy or malice of will. Formal heresy is not only an error of the intellect regarding the assent given to the objective heresy, but also a sin in the will on account of the pertinacity conjoined to the error. A final distinction of heresy may be made into internal or mental heresy, and external heresy. Internal heresy consists in merely internal acts of the intellect resulting from any erroneous judgment concerning an objective heresy, and which is not externally manifested by any obstinate words or signs or deeds. External heresy consists in a sufficiently outward manifestation, expressed in words, signs or equivalent actions of the internal heresy.

From the divisions just given, properly speaking, only external heresy, which constitutes a crime in the external forum, is subject to ecclesiastical penalties.

9. Blat, "*Commentarium Textus Codicis Iuris Canonici,*" III, §I, tit 1. p. 58.

The crime of heresy can be committed only by one baptized. For, although Baptism is not required that one be guilty of infidelity before God, if he dissent to the revealed truth which has been sufficiently proposed, nevertheless, one cannot be called a rebel to the Church's authority who is not subject to it, nor can the Church inflict penalties or exercise judgment against a man who, through Baptism, is not already subject to the Church. To constitute the crime of heresy objectively, it is necessary that one stubbornly deny a revealed truth or a dogma or article of faith declared or defined by the Church. Hence, whoever does not believe a private revelation or even a revelation made to the universal Church, but not yet sufficiently defined as a dogma by the Church, does not incur the crime of heresy and therefore become comprehended by the canonical definition of heretic.[10]

In canon 1325, 2, a heretic is defined as one who, having received Baptism and retaining the name of Christian, obstinately denies or entertains doubts concerning any of the truths of the Divine Catholic faith.

SCHISM: A schismatic may be described as one who cuts himself off from the unity of the Church, inasmuch as this unity consists in the communion of the faithful between themselves and in the subjection due the Roman Pontiff.[11]

This separation from the Church must be by deliberate act on the part of the schismatic himself, or by the community to which he ascribes himself. Hence, if one who has committed a serious crime, has been punished by a separation from the communion of the faithful, he would be called an excommunicant, not a schismatic. Hence, schism involves a twofold act: a withdrawal from the fold of the Church, and a stubborn

10. Wernz, "*Jus Decretalium,*" VI, 281.
11. canon 1325, §2.

refusal to acknowledge the supreme authority of the Roman Pontiff, as the Vicar of Christ, and the supreme pastor of the faithful.

Schism, strictly speaking, confines itself to the rejection of obedience to the Roman Pontiff, but does not impugn or deny any of the dogmas of Faith. Not infrequently, however, this withdrawal from the obedience to the Pope is mixed with the denial of some dogma, and so, to the crime of schism is adjoined the delinquency of heresy. The division between occult schism and manifest schism is of no moment, since, in the canon law, only schism which is manifested and consummated by an external act is subject to ecclesiastical penalty. To perpetrate the crime of schism it is necessary that one either expressly and directly, or indirectly withdraw himself from the obedience of the Roman Pontiff, thus separating himself from the other members of the Catholic communion; that this withdrawal be conjoined with pertinacity; thirdly, that the withdrawal be from those things by which the unity of the Church is constituted. One would not incur schism by the mere transgression of a Pontifical law, otherwise every violator of the laws of the Universal Church would be considered a schismatic, which is absurd. Nor could we call those schismatics, who refuse obedience to the Roman Pontiff because of a reasonable doubt concerning the validity of his election to that office, or those who would refuse obedience to the Pope as a civil power, not as Pastor of the Church.[12]

The crime of heresy or schism, alone, however, does not necessarily make one a member of an heretical or schismatical sect. A sect may be described as a group of Christians who, banded together, refuse to accept the

---

12. Wernz, "*Jus Decretalium*," VI, 354.

supreme authority or teaching of the Catholic Church.[13] They constitute merely a religious party under human unauthorized leadership, or a sect. Hence, the term sect connotes a group of individual heretics or schismatics morally united by a common bond of belief or purpose. And it is only when one becomes affiliated with such, and not merely by the crime of heresy or schism, that he is considered as a member of an heretical or schismatical sect. But even though one guilty of heresy or schism be not a member of a sect, he is equally disqualified from validly acting as a sponsor if he has been declared excommunicated by condemnatory or declaratory sentence because of his heresy or schism.[14]

The words *sententia condemnatoria vel declaratoria* are to be carefully noted in this canon. By a sentence is meant a legitimate pronouncement by which a judge defines or decides a cause proposed by the contending parties, which has been dealt with according to the prescriptions of the law. The sentence is called definitive if it decides the principal cause, or interlocutory if it decides other causes, relative or incidental to the principal cause.[15] In criminal trials, a definitive sentence is said to be condemnatory when the penalty is pronounced by the judge; it is called declaratory when the judge defines that the defendant has incurred the penalty already specified in the law. For instance, by canon 2326, those who manufacture false relics, or knowingly sell or distribute them, or have them exposed

---

13. "In the Acts of the Apostles the word sect is applied to the religious tendency with which one has identified himself (Acts, XXIV, 5; XXVI, 5; XXVIII, 22). St. Peter speaks of 'lying teachers who shall bring in sects of perdition.' In subsequent Catholic ecclesiastical usage this meaning was retained. Hence, a sect may be described a group of Christians, who, banded together, refuse to accept the teaching and supreme authority of the Catholic Church." Catholic Encyclopedia, vol. XIII, article "Sects."

14. canon 765, §2.

15. canon 1686, §1.

to the public veneration of the faithful, *ipso facto* incur excommunication reserved to the Ordinary. This penalty is *latae sententiae.* If one should be guilty of such a crime, by the very commission of it, he would simultaneously incur the penalty annexed to this violation. Hence, if one were tried on this indictment in an ecclesiastical court, and adjudged guilty, the sentence of the judge would not inflict the penalty, for from the moment the crime was committed the penalty was incurred; but the judge's sentence juridically makes manifest the existence of this crime and the consequent penalty already annexed to it by law. This is what is known as a declaratory sentence.

A condemnatory sentence, however, is one which pronounces the defendant guilty of the offense for which he has been indicted, and formally pronounces the penal sentence prescribed by the law for such a violation. For example, canon 2328 declares that whoever desecrates corpses, or graves of the dead, to commit theft or from some other evil motive, is to be punished with personal interdict, is *ipso facto* infamous, and if such a one be a cleric, he should be deposed. Such a crime would render the offender infamous by law, *lata sententia.* The other two penalties of personal interdict for either laymen or clerics, and deposition if the transgressor be a cleric, are *sententiae ferendae.* Hence, that one incur these latter penalties, his guilt must be formally pronounced by a competent ecclesiastical court, and sentenced to the penalties with which the law punishes such violations.

Even though one has committed a crime, the penalty for which renders him liable to excommunication, or infamy by law, or exclusion from legitimate acts, whether these penalties be *latae* or *ferendae sententiae,* he is not thereby debarred from acting as sponsor under pain of nullity unless these penalties have been declared or inflicted by a declaratory or condemnatory sentence.

Another means by which a declaratory or condemnatory sentence may be imposed is by way of particular precept. Such a sentence should be pronounced in writing, or in the presence of two witnesses, and should contain the reasons for which the penalty is inflicted.[16]

Excommunicati.

The Church, by its Divine foundation, is a perfect society. It is, therefore, not only entitled to place certain conditions for admittance into its membership, but, like any other organization, has the power to deprive unworthy members of the rights and privileges of membership. Censure is the generic term denoting a penalty by which a baptized person, delinquent and contumacious, is deprived of certain spiritual goods, or goods connected with spiritual ones, until he has given up his contumacy and obtained absolution.[17] Excommunication is a censure excluding a person from the communion of the faithful and depriving him of certain spiritual rights enumerated in Church law.[18]

Censures are reserved or not reserved according as the faculty to absolve therefrom is, or is not, withheld from persons ordinarily having absolution faculties. According to the gravity of the crime, censures may be reserved to the Ordinary, or to the Apostolic See.

Excommunication reserved to the Holy See *specialissimo modo* is incurred by:

1. Whoever desecrates or casts away the Sacred Species, or carries them away, or retains them for an evil purpose (c. 2320).

2. Whoever violently assaults the person of the Roman Pontiff (c. 2343, §1).

3. Whoever absolves or feigns to absolve an accom-

16. canon 2225.
17. canon 2241, §1.
18. canon 2257.

plice in a grievous sin against the sixth commandment (c. 2367, §1).

4. Whoever dares to directly violate the sacramental seal of confession (c. 2369, §1).

Excommunication reserved to the Holy See *speciali modo* is incurred by:

1. Apostates, heretics and schismatics (c. 2314, §1).

2. Editors and publishers of books of apostates, heretics and schismatics who propound and defend apostasy, heresy and schism. Likewise those who read or retain knowingly, and without due permission, such books or any other book prohibited by name through a Pontifical pronouncement (c. 2318).

3. Those not ordained priests who feign to say Mass, or hear confession (c. 2322, §1).

4. Persons who appeal from the laws, decrees or mandates of the Pope to an ecumenical council (c. 2332).

5. Those who have recourse to the civil powers to impede the communications, or orders of the Apostolic See or its Legates, or who prohibit directly or indirectly their promulgation or execution (c. 2333).

6. Those who enact laws or decrees contrary to the liberty of Church's rights (c. 2334, §1).

7. Those who impede directly or indirectly the exercise of ecclesiastical jurisdiction by having recourse to the civil power (c. 2334, §2).

8. Whoever dares to indict before a civil magistrate, a Cardinal or Legate of the Apostolic See, or a major official of the Roman Curia, or his own Ordinary (c. 2341).

9. Those who violate the person of a cardinal, a Papal Legate, archbishop or bishop (c. 2343, §§2 and 3).

10. Usurpers of the goods and rights of the Roman Church (c. 2345).

11. Forgers and falsifiers of Papal documents, or those who knowingly use the same (c. 2360).

12. Those who make a false denunciation of a confessor before an ecclesiastical Superior of the crime of solicitation (c. 2363).

Excommunication reserved *simpliciter* to the Holy See is incurred by:

1. Those who traffic in indulgences (c. 2327).
2. Those enrolled in masonic sects, or in other societies of similar nature which plot against the Church, or against lawful civil authority (c. 2335).
3. Whoever knowingly presumes to absolve from an excommunication *latae sententiae* reserved to the Pope either *speciali modo* or *specialissimo modo* (c. 2338, §1).
4. Those who proffer aid or favor to an *excommunicatus vitandus* in his crime (c. 2338, §2).
5. Those who cite before a civil tribunal without permission of the Apostolic See, a bishop or an abbot, a Prelate *nullius*, or the Superior General of a religious order approved by the Pope (c. 2341).
6. Violators of the Cloister of Nuns with solemn vows (c. 2342).
7. Those who presume to expropriate ecclesiastical goods of any kind, or who prevent the income or revenues of these goods from going to those entitled thereto (c. 2346).
8. Those who engage in duelling and those who cooperate therein (c. 2351).
9. Clerics in major orders or Religious with solemn vows who attempt marriage, even civilly, and their consorts (c. 2388, §1).
10. Those who obtain by simony, any ecclesiastical offices, benefices or dignities (c. 2392).
11. Those who remove or destroy or conceal or substantially alter any document belonging to the Episcopal Curia (c. 2405).

Excommunication reserved to the Ordinary is incurred by:

1. Catholics who give matrimonial consent before a non-Catholic minister against the prescriptions of canon 1063, §1 (c. 2319, §1).

2. Those who manufacture or knowingly sell or distribute or expose to public veneration, false relics (c. 2326).

3. Catholics who, at the time of their marriage, agree to have all their children, or some of them, educated outside the Catholic Church (c. 2319, §2).

4. Those who knowingly dare to offer their children to non-Catholic ministers for Baptism (c. 2319, §3).

5. Parents or guardians who knowingly have their children instructed or reared in a non-Catholic denomination (c. 2319, §4).

6. Those who violate the person of clerics below the rank of bishop, or of Regulars of either sex (c. 2343, 4).

7. Those who successfully procure abortion (c. 2350, §1).

8. Religious who apostasize from their religious organization (c. 2385).

9. Professed religious by simple perpetual vows, who contract marriage, even civilly, and their consorts (c. 2388, §2).

Excommunication, *nemini* reserved, is incurred by:

1. Publishers and authors who print books of Sacred Scripture, or annotations and commentaries thereon, without due permission (c. 2318, §2).

2. Those who command or compel the ecclesiastical burial of infidels, apostates, heretics, of those excommunicated by name, or those under interdict (c. 2339).

3. Those who alienate ecclesiastical property without Papal permission when such is required (c. 2347, 3).

4. Those who coerce a person by any means to embrace the clerical or religious state, or to take religious vows (c. 2352).

5. Penitents who fail or neglect to denounce a confessor guilty of solicitation, to the proper authorities within a month (c. 2368, §2).

Infames infamia iuris.

By infamy is meant the privation or diminution of one's good name or reputation resulting from a fault that is serious, and attended in many cases with public contempt.[19] A person may become canonically infamous in two ways: by a disposition of the ecclesiastical law which pronounces him such on account of some crime; this is infamy of law (*infamia iuris*). Or he may become infamous by his own evil deeds which cause the loss of his good name among upright and serious minded men, even though the evil deeds are not expressly mentioned by the law, or no sentence of infamy has been declared against the transgressor.[20] This is known as infamy of fact (*infamia facti.*) Whether and when infamy of fact is incurred, is for the Ordinary to decide.[21] Infamy of law ceases only by a dispensation granted by the Holy See.[22] Infamy of fact ceases when, in the prudent estimation of the Ordinary, the reputation of the delinquent has been sufficiently reestablished among upright and serious minded people. This depends upon particular circumstances, the good behavior of the delinquent, and a general conduct indicative of enduring amendment, concerning all of which the Ordinary shall decide.

Infamy of law is incurred by:

1. Catholics who formally enroll their names in a non-Catholic sect, or who publicly adhere to such (c. 2314, §§1, 2 and 3).

2. Those who desecrate the Sacred Species, or for an evil purpose carry them away, or keep them (c. 2320).

19. Wernz, "*Jus Decretalium,*" VI, 105.
20. Wernz, "*Jus Decretalium,*" VI, 105.
21. Augustine, "*Commentary on Canon Law,*" VIII, p. 246.
22. canon 2295.

3. Whoever desecrates the corpses or graves of the dead to commit theft, or for some other evil motive (c. 2328).

4. Persons laying violent hands on the person of the Pope, of cardinals or Papal Legates (c. 2343, §1, n. 2 and §2, n. 2).

5. Those who engage in a duel, and their seconds (c. 2351, §2).

6. Whoever, bound by the matrimonial bond, attempts another marriage, even though it be only a civil marriage (c. 2356).

7. Laymen who have been lawfully convicted of crimes against the sixth commandment committed with minors of either sex who have not yet reached the sixteenth year of age; and also those who have been lawfully condemned for fornication, sodomy, incest or panderage (c. 2357, §1).

Actus legitimi.

By legitimate or legal ecclesiastical acts are understood: the office of administrator of ecclesiastical property, the functions of those persons in the ecclesiastical court acting in the capacity of judge, auditor, relator, defender of the bond of marriage or ordination, fiscal promoter and promoter of faith, notary, chancellor, cursor, apparitor, lawyer or procurator in ecclesiastical causes, the office of sponsor for the sacraments of Baptism and Confirmation, voting in ecclesiastical elections, and the exercising of the right of patronage.[23]

Those who have incurred infamy of law, are disqualified for the valid exercise of legitimate ecclesiastical acts (c. 2294, §1); those who have incurred infamy of fact are forbidden the licit exercise of these legitimate ecclesiastical acts (c. 2294, 2). Others prohibited the lawful or licit exercise of legitimate ecclesiastical acts

---

23. canon 2256, §2.

are those who have rendered themselves suspected of heresy (c. 2315); those who have attempted suicide (c. 2350, §2) and those guilty of the public crimes of adultery and public concubinage, or those who have been lawfully condemned for other serious offenses against the sixth commandment until they shall have manifested sincere repentence and amendment. Those disqualified for the valid exercise of legitimate ecclesiastical acts, besides those who are infamous by infamy of law, are:

1. Those against whom a sentence of excommunication has been pronounced (c. 2263).

2. Anyone who, by violence or deceit, abducts a woman against her will, either with the intention of marrying her, or for the purpose of sensual gratification; or who abducts a girl not yet of age, even though she is willing, without the knowledge or against the consent of her parents or guardians (c. 2353).

3. Layman who have been lawfully condemned for homicide, the abduction of persons of either sex under the age of puberty, selling a man into servitude, or for some other evil purpose; usury, as understood and condemned by modern legislation; plunder or violent theft; grand larceny, whether qualified or unqualified; incendiarism or malicious destruction of property of considerably great value; serious mutilation or wounding, or assault (c. 2354, §1).

4. Religious of perpetual vows, whether solemn or simple, who unlawfully leave the religious house with the intention of not returning; or who, having lawfully left the house, do not return to it, with the intention of withdrawing from religious obedience (c. 2385).

Nec sit clericus depositus vel degradatus.

Deposition and degradation are vindictive ecclesiastical penalties imposed on clerics only in punishment for some serious offense.[24] These penalties can be imposed only for the perpetration of crimes expressly mentioned in the Code.[25] There is no crime mentioned in the Code for which the penalties of deposition and degradation are incurred *latae sententiae;* hence, they can be inflicted only by a condemnatory sentence, and cases involving their declaration are to be tried before a tribunal of five judges.[26] The penalty of deposition may be inflicted on—obstinate apostates, heretics and schismatics after repeated admonitions (c. 2314); clerics who desecrate the Sacred Species (c. 2320), who simulate the celebration of Mass or the hearing of sacramental confessions (c. 2322), who violate the graves of the dead (c. 2328), who are guilty of procuring abortion (c. 2350, §1), or of certain very grave delinguencies, such as murder, abduction of young children, usury, incendiarism, slave traffic, theft, etc. (c. 2354, §2); clerics in Sacred Orders who obstinately refuse for three months to wear the clerical dress or give up a mode of life unbecoming to their state (c. 2379), who illegally enter into possession of a benefice (c. 2394, §2); who, in spite of several admonitions, continue to hold a benefice, office or dignity of which they have been deprived (c. 2401).

Degradation includes deposition, perpetual privation of the ecclesiastical dress and reduction of the cleric to the status of a layman, which implies the loss of clerical privileges (c. 2305, §1). A degraded cleric is not thereby exempted from the obligations of celibacy, or of reciting the Breviary.[27] By the present legislation, degradation may be inflicted on clerics only for crimes expressed in law, and only on those who, having been already deposed and deprived of the clerical habit, continue for a year to give great scandal. This penalty is

24. canon 2298, nn. 10 and 12.
25. canons 2303, §3, and 2305, §2.
26. canon 1576, §1, n. 2.
27. Vermeersch, "*Epitome Iuris Canonici,*" III, 499.

inflicted on clerics who have formally joined or publicly adhered to a non-Catholic sect and do not amend after warning (c. 2314), on those who lay violent hands on the Sovereign Pontiff (c. 2343) or who are guilty of voluntary homicide (c. 2354), or of particularly grave cases of solicitation (c. 268), on Religious bound by a solemn vow of chastity, or on clerics in Sacred Orders who presume to contract marriage and refuse to heed warning (c. 2388). The penalty is always *ferendae sententiae.*"

The father and mother, the husband or the wife of the one to be baptized are disqualified from validly functioning as sponsor. Although the above mentioned were forbidden to act as sponsor by the canon law which obtained before the Code, this prohibition did not bind under pain of nullity. By virtue of the present discipline, however, they become wholly incompetent. The motive prompting this prohibition seems to be founded in one of the reasons for having a sponsor. For it is the duty of the sponsor to watch over the moral and religious education of his spiritual protégé when those on whom this obligation is primarily incumbent, fail. The incongruity, however, of having both the primary and secondary obligation resident in the same persons, is evident. For, if the parents, through death or negligence, have not provided for the religious upbringing of their offspring, there is no definite obligation upon anyone to rear the child in the Catholic faith. Moreover, this obligation is already incumbent upon the parents by reason of their natural parentage, and it is to provide against the spiritual abandonment of the child that a sponsor is required. Furthermore, it seems that parents who are so recreant to the duty imposed by natural law of providing for the religious training of their progeny, would feel little compunction in disregarding an obligation imposed by an ecclesiastical precept. An added reason for this disqualification can be sought in the legislation prior to the Code, in virtue of which the diriment impediment of spiritual relationship arose between the sponsor and the parents of the one baptized. Hence, if a parent acted as sponsor, he automatically contracted this impediment with his consort. This complication gave rise to the question whether such relationship brought with it the loss of the right to the marital relations.[28]

The consort is excluded from the office of sponsor, because of the apparent unbecomingness of the use of marriage after the contraction of spiritual relationship.[29] It seems further incongruous that one of the two, so intimately united in marriage, should also stand in the relation of spiritual parent to the other. A warning would not be inadvisable in regard to the Baptism of converts immediately before marriage. A priest should not allow the betrothed to act as sponsor at this Baptism —an action which would immediately beget the impediment of spiritual relationship.

The fourth requisite for the validity of sponsorship is the actual selection or designation of the person or persons for this office. Such selection must be made prior to the ceremony, and subsequent ratification is totally insufficient.[30] The subject of the sacrament has the primary right to select his sponsor. Of course, this presupposes that the baptismal candidate be competent to make such a selection. Hence, he must be of a sufficient age to perform a rational selection. If he has already attained his majority (c. 89) there is no question—but a difficulty arises if the child is a minor. Vlaming holds that he must have completed his fourteenth year.[31] He

28. Schmalzgrueber, "*Jus Universum Ecclesiasticum,*" lib IV, tit XI, nn. 42-49.
29. Vlaming, "*Praelectiones Iuris Matrimonii,*" I, 381.
30. Augustine, "*Commentary on Canon Law,*" vol. IV, p. 79.
31. Vlaming, "*Praelectiones Iuris Matrimonii,*" I, 382.

bases his contention on the right of personal action granted to minors over fourteen years of age (c. 1648, §3) in spiritual causes, and likewise from the fact that fourteen is a sufficient age for the legitimacy of sponsorship (c. 766, §1). If the child is incompetent because of infancy or imbecility, the privilege and duty of choosing the sponsor rests on the parents or guardians of the candidate. No matter what ecclesiastical punishment has been inflicted upon them, they are not deprived of this right.[32] Nevertheless, they are bound to select for sponsor a person who has all the requirements for liceity and validity. Should they select one who may validly but not licitly act in this capacity, it is the right of the pastor to reject him, although if such a person does actually go through the ceremony, he contracts the spiritual relationship and becomes a true sponsor.[33]

Finally, if the child or his parents and guardians fail, the right of selection falls on the minister, whether he be Ordinary or Extraordinary. Failure on the part of the parents consists in refusal or neglect to provide any sponsors for the child. Tantamount to failure is the obstinate insistence of the parents on the appointment of a person who could not validly act an sponsor. In such a case, the parents are truly deficient.

The final requisite for the valid functioning as a sponsor, is physical touch in the actual baptismal ablution. Four terms are used to denote the physical act whereby sponsors act in their official capacity—*Tenere, i. e.,* to hold the child in the act of Baptism, when the water is poured on the head; *tangere,* to touch the child on the arm or any other part of the body whilst another holds it over the baptismal font; *levare,* to lift or raise out of the water when Baptism has been administered

32. Vlaming, "*Praelectiones Iuris Matrimonii,*" I, 382.
33. Cappello, "*De Sacramentis,*" III, 562.

by immersion; *suscipere,* to receive from the baptismal font, or from the hands of the minister.

An instruction on the force of the word *tenere* was given by the Congregation of the Propagation of the Faith[34] on Jan. 21, 1856: *"Per verba (Ritualis) 'patrino infantem tenente' haud susceptio absoluta requiritur, cum 'tenere' aeque intelligatur ac sufficiat, si patrinus, ut in more est, physico contactu infantis jungat se cum eo cujus manibus ille tenetur, et ad aquae infusionem comitetur deferentem, quin opus sit ut patrinus vel matrina tantum, amoto deferente, infantem suas in manus excipiens, sacerdoti baptizandum exhibeat."* It is not necessary, then, that the sponsor actually hold the child during the baptismal ablution, but it is sufficient to join himself by physical contact with the infant, such as placing his hand on the child. But the assertion of Augustine,[35] that it is sufficient that the sponsor put his or her arm in that of the person who holds the child, or touch that person, *v. g.*, nurse or midwife, and accompany him or her to the baptismal font. Whence it may be concluded that mediate physical contact is sufficient"—does not seem to be warranted by the words of the above instruction.

A sponsor may be said truly to fulfill this requirement by touching the child's clothes during the actual baptismal ceremony, or by receiving the child from the minister of the sacrament immediately after the ceremony.[36]

The actual participation of the sponsor at the baptismal ceremony may be performed through a proxy. Although there are certain positive prerogatives required of one who would validly act as sponsor, nevertheless, nothing more than the use of reason and legitimate deputation is demanded of a proxy. Deputa-

34. Collectanea S. C. de Prop. Fide, n. 1119.
35. Augustine, *"Commentary on Canon Law,"* IV, p. 80.
36. Cappello, *"De Sacramentis,"* III, 563.

tion of a proxy can be oral or written. There is no special form required by the Code. It should be expressly given before the Baptism. Subsequent ratification would be insufficient. Although the reputation is revocable, the revocation is not effective until such is made known to the proxy.[37]

The Code proceeds logically from an enumeration of the requirements for validly acting as sponsor to a treatment of the requisites for liceity. In this regard the legal requirements are given under five headings.

The first requisite is that of age. This seems to be a further determination of the Roman Ritual's prescription,[38] *"Hos autem patrinos saltem in aetate pubertatis . . . maxime convenit."* The Code specifies that the sponsor shall have reached his fourteenth year of age. It is to be noted that the law does not demand the completion of the fourteenth year, but merely its inception. This prescription admits of exception for any just cause. Such a cause would be the extraordinary moral or intellectual qualities of the proposed sponsor, family traditions, etc. The minister of the sacrament, and not necessarily the pastor, is the competent judge to determine and decide the cogency of this reason.

Under the second heading the Code debars from lawful participation in the office of sponsor those whose moral character and reputation indicate a want of fitness to discharge the solemn office.

Propter notorium delictum.

In ecclesiastical law a delict is an external and morally imputable transgression of a law to which there

37. Cappello, *"De Sacramentis,"* III, 563.
38. Tit II, cap 1, n. 24.

has been attached at least an indefinite canonical penalty (c. 2195, §1). A delict becomes notorious by notoriety of law if adjudged officially in a court of law (c. 1902, §4), or if it has been confessed in a judicial manner (c. 1750). It is notorious by fact when it is a matter of public knowledge, and has been committed in such adjuncts that its concealment by any artifice or chicanery is impossible. Consequently, not alone the deed, but also the criminal nature of the deed, must be notorious. Yet neither notoriety of fact nor of law is sufficient of itself to exclude one from lawfully assuming the office of sponsor, but there is further required that he be on that very account excommunicated, excluded from legitimate acts, or infamous by infamy of law.[39]

Unlike the prescription regarding validity, there is not here required the intenvention of a sentence declaring the culprit bound by such penalty. The crimes for which a delinquent may have incurred the penalties of excommunication, exclusion from legitimate ecclesiastical acts or become infamous by infamy of law, have been enumerated in commenting on the preceding canon. There is no mention made here of a deposed or degraded cleric, because these pealties are always *ferendae sententiae.* This connotes the intervention of a condemnatory sentence, which would prevent even the valid assumption of this office.

Nec sit interdictus.

Interdict is incurred by:

1. Those who desecrate corpses or graves of the dead to commit theft, or for some other evil motive (c. 2328).

2. Those who celebrate or cause to be celebrated, divine offices in interdicted places (c. 2338, §3).

---

39. Blat, "*Commentarium Textus Codicis,*" III, §I, tit I, p. 59.

3. Those who were the cause of a local interdict, or an interdict in a community (c. 2338, §4).

4. Those who give ecclesiastical sepulture to infidels, apostates, heretics or schismatics (c. 2339).

5. Those who, though validly married, attempt another marriage, and after warning from the Ordinary, continue to live in unlawful relationship (c. 2356).

The prohibition to lawfully act as sponsor is extended to those who in any other way are publicly considered criminal, or who have become infamous by the infamy of fact. A crime is considered public if it has already been divulged, or has been committed in such circumstances that it can be prudently judged that the knowledge of it will soon become known (c. 2197). Infamy of fact imports the loss of one's good reputation among upright men of sound judgment because of some sin or vice (c. 2293, §3).

Fidei Rudimenta Noverit.

The third requirement postulates a knowledge by the sponsor of the rudiments of the Catholic religion. By rudiments of the faith are to be understood the principal mysteries, namely, the Incarnation and the Blssed Trinity, the Lord's Prayer, the Apostles' Creed, the acts of Faith, Hope and Charity, the Ten Commandments, the Precepts of the Church and the effects of Baptism.[40] The reason for demanding this knowledge in the sponsor is evident. The Roman Ritual and Code prescribe, among the sponsor's duties, the obligation of instructing the one baptized in the truths of the Catholic faith.[41]

Neither a novice nor a professed member of any religious institute can lawfully act as sponsor unless in case of necessity, and with the express permission of,

40. S. C. de Prop. Fide, 18 Oct., 1883; Collectanea, n. 1606, n. 17.
41. Roman Ritual, tit II, cap 1, n. 25; canon 769.

at least, the local Superior. By a religious institute is meant a society approved by legitimate ecclesiastical authority, whose members strive after evangelical perfection by observing the special laws of that society and by making public vows, either temporal or perpetual, the former to be renewed when the time of them expires (c. 488, §1). A novice is one who has become an acknowledged subject of a religious society, either by the reception of the religious habit, or in any other manner prescribed by the constitutions of that society (c. 553). A professed religious is one who, after the completion of his novitiate, consecrates himself to God through three vows, and to the service of the community to which he is ascribed.[42] It is to be noted that a professed religious who has been lawfully dismissed or absolved from his vows, or secularized, ceases to be a religious, and is not comprehended by this prohibition.[43]

The reasons for prohibiting religious to act as sponsors are not hard to find. The obligations consequent to sponsorship are incongruous with religious life, and its retirement from worldly cares. Moreover, the intimacy of the relation between the sponsor and his godchild might not be without its temptations. An exception is made by this paragraph of the canon, in cases where necessity urges, and the express permission of the competent superior has been obtained. The necessity can be either physical or moral. The former is present when there is no other suitable person to be obtained to act as sponsor, and the latter when a refusal would beget serious moral results, for instance, the violent displeasure of the parents. The judge of these circumstances will be the local religious Superior, whose permission to act as sponsor must be not presumed, but expressly granted, either verbally or in writing.[44]

---

42. canon 571; Augustine, "*Commentary on Canon Law*," III, p. 251.
43. Blat, *Commentarium Textus Codicis*," III, §I, tit I, p. 60.
44. Blat, "*Commentarium Textus Codicis*," III, §I, tit I, p. 60.

The fifth requirement is that the sponsor be not a cleric in Sacred Orders, unless he have the expressed permission of his Ordinary. Included by terms "Sacred Orders," are those who have received sub-deaconship, deaconship and priesthood.[45] Hence, seminarians or clerics in minor orders are not included by this prohibition. However, those in Sacred Orders may lawfully act as sponsor with express—not presumed—permission of their own proper Ordinary. This Ordinary is the one into whose diocese or territory the cleric has been incardinated.[46] The term Ordinary comprehends residential Bishops, Abbots and Prelates *nullius*, Vicars-general, Administrators, Vicars-apostolic, Prefects-apostolic (c. 198, §1).

When there is a doubt whether one has the essential qualifications to function validly or licitly as sponsor, recourse must be had to the Ordinary, if time permit. This prescription is contained in canon 767. *"In dubio utrum quis valide vel licite admitti possit, necne, ad patrini munus, parochus, si tempus suppetat, consulat Ordinarium."* This recourse must be had when the doubt is one either of law or of fact.[47] The clause *si tempus suppetat* is to be construed as the time which would be consumed for any ordinary means of communication. The use of the telegraph or the telephone are considered extraordinary means.[48] Hence, the time for communication with the Ordinary would be computed according to the usual time required for personal journey, or letter.

When such recourse is resorted to, it becomes the duty of the Ordinary to decide on the admissibility of the proposed sponsor. If it is certain to the Ordinary that the sponsor lacks a qualification for the valid or

45. canon 949.
46. Blat, "*Commentarium Textus Codicis*," III, §I, tit I, p. 60.
47. Blat, "*Commentarium Textus Codicis*," III, §I, tit I, p. 60.
48. Vermeersch, "*Epitome Iuris Canonici*," II, 353.

licit assumption of this office, then he must forbid the admission of such a one as sponsor, for by the common law of the Church, he has no faculty to dispense. If, however, in a particular case, where a just cause were present, and recourse to the Holy See were difficult, while at the same time there was grave danger in delay, the Ordinary, by virtue of canon 81, could dispense from such qualifications as are usually dispensed by the Holy See. When, however, the doubt concerning the qualifications of the sponsor perdures in the mind of the Ordinary, the provisions of canon 15 are to be invoked. Hence, if the doubt be one of law, the prohibition ceases; if it be one of fact, the Ordinary is empowered to dispense, provided the dispensation be from a qualification usually granted by the Roman Pontiff. When time does not admit of recourse to the Ordinary, the pastor—not the minister of the sacrament—may, if the doubt be one of law, take advantage of canon 15, and admit the sponsor. If the doubt be one of fact, he can for a just reason presume a dispensation of the Ordinary.[49]

49. Blat, "*Commentarium Textus Codicis,*" III, §I, tit I, p. 61.

CHAPTER VIII

The Extent of Spiritual Relationship and the Duties of Sponsors

The extent of the spiritual relationship arising from Baptism is defined by canon 768, which reads: "*Ex baptismo spiritualem cognationem contrahunt tantum cum baptizato, baptizans et patrinus.*"

Spiritual relationship is a supernatural bond which, by virtue of ecclesiastical law, establishes a connection between certain persons through the reception or the administration of Baptism and of Confirmation.[1] Since by Baptism, a man is born anew, that is, regenerated in the spiritual life, consequently, just as the natural parents contract with their child a natural relationship, those who participate in the spiritual regeneration, contract with him a spiritual relationship. One of the effects of this spiritual relationship is a diriment impediment to matrimony.

The notion of spiritual paternity asserted itself in the very beginning of Apostolic times. Saint Peter refers to "my son, Mark;"[2] Timothy is addressed as "my son" by Saint Paul,[3] by reason of the spiritual relationship begotten through Baptism.[4] The origin of spiritual relationship as a matrimonial impediment is based solely on ecclesiastical law.[5] The viewpoint of the early Christians toward marriages between persons thus spiritually related, was one of great antipathy. As

1. Petrovits, "*New Church Law on Matrimony,*" p. 379.
2. I St. Peter, V, 13.
3. II Timothy, II, 1.
4. Cappello, "*De Sacramentis,*" III, 568.
5. Schmalzgrueber, "*Jus Ecclesiasticum Universum,*" lib IV, §III, tit XI, n. 2.

a result, custom gradually gave rise to the prohibition of such marriages under pain of nullity. The first written law forbidding marriage between those spiritually related was enacted by the Emperor Justinian in the year 530; "*Ea persona omnimodo ad nuptias venire prohibenda, quam aliquis, sive alumna sit, sive non, a sacrosancto suscepit baptismate; cum nihil aliud sic inducere potest paternam affectionem, et justam nuptiarum prohibitionem, quam hujusmodi nexus, per quem, Deo mediante, animae eorum copulatate sunt.*"[6] Though this civil law, as such, did not directly affect the baptized, nevertheless, it reflects the spirit of the age, and is an indication that at that early date this impediment was recognized by the canon law.[7]

A century and a half later, the Council of Trullo, incorporated in its canons this law of the Emperor: "*Quoniam spiritualis necessitudo seu affinitas, corporum conjunctione major est, in nonnullis autem locis cognovimus quosdam qui ex sancto et salutare baptismate infantes suscipiunt, postea quoque cum matribus illorum viduis matrimonium contrahere, statuimus ut in posterum nihil fiat hujusmodi. Si qui autem post praesentem canonem hoc facere deprehensi fuerint, ii quidem primo ab hoc illicito matrimonio desistant, deinde et fornicatorum poenis subjiciantur.*"[8] A Council of Rome held in the year 721 punished by anathema, those who dared to contract marriage when spiritually related: "*Si quis commatrem spiritualem duxerit in conjugium, anathema sit.*"[9] Another council convened at Rome in the year 743, legislated: "*Ut prebyterum, . . . vel etiam spiritualem commatrem, nullus sibi praesumat nefario conjugio copulare. Nam qui hujusmodi opus perpet-*

6. Codex Justiniani, lib V, tit IV, de nuptiis, leg. 26.
7. Benedict XIV, "*De Synodo Dioecesana,*" lib IX, cap X, n. 6.
8. Ss. Concilia, tom IV, 1168.
9. Concil. Roman., can. 4; Ss. Concilia, tom VI, 1456.

raverit, sciat se anathematis vinculo esse obligatum, et Dei judicio condemnatum."[10]

The impediment of spiritual relationship has passed through various stages of development in the course of its history, which may be divided into three distinct periods, namely, the legislation that obtained prior to the Council of Trent; that, from the Council of Trent to the Code, and the present discipline of the Code. Before the Council of Trent the ramifications of spiritual relationship were numerous and involved.

Paternity was the first degree of spiritual relationship arising from the conferring of the sacraments of Baptism and Confirmation. This paternity might be direct or indirect. Direct paternity arose, 1), between the minister of the sacrament and the recipient; 2), between the recipient of the sacrament and the sponsor. Indirect paternity arose, 1), between consort, husband or wife of the minister of the sacrament and the recipient; 2), between the recipient and the consort of the sponsor. The reason of this indirect paternity was that husband and wife were considered two persons in one flesh. Hence, a necessary condition for contracting this impediment was that the consorts had carnally known each other prior to the conferring of the Sacrament.[11]

Compaternity was another degree of spiritual relationship that arose. This relation was twofold—direct and indirect. Direct compaternity arose 1), between the minister of the sacrament and the sponsor; 2), between the minister of the sacrament and parents of the recipient; 3), between the recipient's sponsor and the parents of the recipient. Indirect compaternity arose 1), between the parents of the recipient and the consort, wife or husband of the minister of the sacrament; 2), between

10. Concil. Roman., cap 5; Ss. Concilia, tom VI, 1647.
11. Schmalzgrueber, "*Jus Ecclesiasticum Universum,*" lib IV, §III, tit XI, n. 9; Sanchez, lib VII, de Matrimon., disp. 54, n. 1.

the parents of the recipient and the consort of the sponsor. By reason of this relationship the minister of the sacrament, and the sponsor, were called *compatres*, and their wives *commatres*. They were, so to speak, co-parents with the natural parents of the recipient, inasmuch as they participated in the spiritual regeneration of the recipient of the sacrament. Another degree of spiritual relationship which arose was *Fraternitas*. This fraternity arose between 1), the natural children of the minister of the sacrament, and the recipient; 2), between the natural children of the sponsor, and the recipient. All the above relationships constituted diriment matrimonial impediments.[12] The spiritual relationship arising between the catechumen and his sponsor in the ceremony of *catechesis* constituted an impediment which, however, was not diriment.[13]

The Council of Trent narrowed the scope of this impediment by abolishing the relationship of spiritual fraternity, indirect compaternity and indirect paternity; and reducing the number of sponsors to one of either sex, or, at most, one of each. The relationship arising *ex catechismo* was also abrogated. The legislation of Trent is as follows:. "*Docet experientia, propter multitudinem prohibitionum, multoties in casibus prohibitis ignoranter contrahi matrimonia, in quibus vel non sine magno peccato perseveratur, vel ea non sine magno scandalo dirimuntur. Volens itaque sancta Synodus huic incommodo providere, et a cognationis spiritualis impedimento incipiens, statuit ut unus tantum, sive vir sive mulier, juxta sacrorum instituta canonum, vel ad summum unus et una, baptizatum de baptismo suscipiant: inter quos ac baptizatum ipsum, et illius patrem et matrem, nec non inter baptizantem et baptizatum, baptizatique*

12. Schmalzgrueber, "*Jus Ecclesiasticum Universum,*" lib IV, §III, tit XI, n. 11.
13. C. 2, de spirituali cognatione, IV, e, in VI.

patrem et matrem, tantum spiritualis cognatio contrahatur. Parochus antequam ad baptismum conferendum accedat, diligenter ab iis ad quos spectabit, sciscitetur, quam vel quos elegerint, ut baptiszatum de sacro fonte suscipiant: et eum vel eos tantum ad illum suscipiendum admittat, et in libro eorum nomina describat; doceatque eos quam cognationem contraxerint, ne ignorantia ulla excusari valeant. Quod si alii ultra designatos, baptizatum tetigerint, cognationem spiritualem nullo pacto contrahant, constitutionibus in contrarium facientibus, non obstantibus. Si parochi culpa vel negligentia secus factum fuerit arbitrio Ordinarii puniantur."[14]

According to the Tridentine legislation, spiritual relationship in Baptism was contracted only between the sponsors and the godchild; between the sponsors and the parents of the child; between the minister and the one baptized, and finally between the minister and the parents of the one baptized. In like manner, the same relationship which also arose from Confirmation existed between the minister and the person confirmed and his parents, and also between the sponsor and the one confirmed and his parents. The parents of the person baptized or confirmed, are understood to mean his natural parents, whether the child be legitimate or illegitimate. Hence, parents by adoption would not contract this spiritual relationship.[15]

The Code still further modifies the scope of spiritual relationship. According to its discipline, spiritual relationship still arises from the sacraments of Baptism and Confirmation.[16] Nevertheless, only the relationship associated with Baptism constitutes a matrimonial impediment.[17] Furthermore, this impediment is restricted in its extent to a nullification of marriage between the

14. Sess. XXIV, de reformatione, cap II.
15. Wernz, "*Jus Decretalium,*" IV, 487.
16. canons 768 and 797.
17. canon 1097.

recipient of Baptism, on the one side, and the minister of the sacrament and the godparents, on the other.[18] By the disposition of the present discipline, the relationship of compaternity in Baptism, or of compaternity and paternity in Confirmation, no longer constitute a diriment matrimonial impediment. However, the effects of such a relationship contracted before the promulgation of the Code still prevail, for spiritual relationship, not unlike natural relationship, is perpetual.[19] Still, the impediment of this spiritual relationship ceased with the introduction of the Code.[20] An example might be cited to illustrate this point. A person who acted as sponsor for another confirmed before May 19, 1918, commits a sexual sin with parents of that person after the above date; the sin is still one of incest, although the impediment of spiritual relationship has ceased to exist.

Relying mainly on a Tridentine phrase, several theologians in the past have inferred that sponsors in private Baptism do not contract any relationship with the subject of that sacrament. The Council of Trent, they said, called the office of sponsor a *susceptio de sacro fonte.* In private Baptism, no sacred font is used; consequently, in private Baptism, there is no *susceptio de sacro fonte.* Accordingly, there is no office of sponsor. They reinforced this argument with the contention that the *susceptio* as a ceremony was prescribed for solemn Baptism alone, and therefore could beget spiritual relationship only in that kind of sacramental regeneration. The theologians who championed this opinion present a formidable array.[21] Against this phalanx of authority,

---

18. canon 768 and 1097.
19. Cappello, "*De Sacramentis,*" III, 567.
20. "*Comm. Pontif. ad Cod.,*" 2 Jun., 1918; cf. A. A. S., vol. X, p. 346.
21. St. Alphonsus, "*Theologia Moralis,*" lib VI, 149; Sanchez, "*De Matrimonio,*" lib VII, disp. LXII, 14; Diana, §X, tract. XVI, resol. 29; Lemkuhl, tom II, 991; Gury-Ballerini, tom II, 805; Bucceroni, II, 459; et alii.

however, there stands another host of canonists and theologians to do battle for the opposite opinion.[22]

These latter contend that even in a private Baptism the sponsor becomes the spiritual parent of the subject, and they base their tenet on the following considerations: First of all the Council of Trent, when referring to the spiritual relationship contracted by sponsors, makes no distinction between solemn and private Baptism. Again, the Congregation of the Council decided, both in a particular case and as a general principle, that when Baptism is conferred at home without the usual ceremonies, the sponsors, nevertheless, contract spiritual relationship with their godchild.[23]

Some, indeed, would retort with a declaration of the same Congregation under date of May 16, 1711, but that declaration proves only that no spiritual relationship results from the mere supplying of the ceremonies.[24] Consequently the response of March 5, 1678, being a mere interpretation of a pre-existent law, obtained, without any promulgation, the force of law, and retained such legal force, at least until the appearance of the Code.

As a third proof, the canonists of the affirmative side point out the nugatory character of their adversaries' arguments. Cappello goes so far as to accuse these adversaries of tearing a phrase out of its context to suit their purpose; for he asserts that the phrase *de sacro fonte* occurs, not in the place where the Council of Trent makes mention of persons spiritually related, but in another passage where the phrase *de sacro fonte* is used, either because Baptism is usually conferred at the sacred

---

22. Reiffenstuhl, lib IV, tit XI, 14; Feye, n. 413; Suarez, §III, q. 67, art. 8; Pihring, lib IV, tit XI, 36; Schmalzgrueber, lib IV, tit XI, 55; Gasparri, I, 836; et alii.

23. S. C. Concil., 5 Mar., 1678; cf. Cappello, "*De Sacramentis,*" III, 559; Gasparri, "*De Matrimonio,*" 836; Wernz, "*Jus Decretalium,*" IV, 489.

24. Gasparri, "*De Matrimonio,*" I, 836; Wernz, "*Jus Decretalium,*" IV, 489, note 48; Cappello, "*De Sacramentis,*" III, 559, note 15.

font, or because the word font is used figuratively for the sacrament conferred at it.[25]

The final argument is drawn from the nature of the sponsor's office. Sponsorship is something more than a mere ceremony; it is an office, or function, of lifelong duration, a function of no less advantage to a child baptized privately than to a child baptized at the font in a church. It is true that St. Alphonsus called the contrary or negative opinion the more probable one,[26] but it is equally true that even this prince of moralists was not infallible, and that in all likelihood he was unaware of the decree of March 5, 1678.[27]

Such was the state of the question before the promulgation of the Code; St. Alphonsus and a number of prominent theologians, against a particular declaration of the Sacred Congregation of the Council, and a host of canonists. The Code seems to solve the difficulty. But it is a remarkable fact that so eminent a canonist as Vermeersch questions the existence of spiritual relationship between the subject and the sponsors at a private Baptism.[28] The same author, however, seems to contradict this statement in commenting on matrimony, when he says that the impediment of spiritual relationship probably is contracted by the sponsor and his godchild at a private Baptism.[29]

Cappello, on the contrary, affirms that the sponsor, even in a private Baptism, becomes the spiritual relative of the person baptized. He seems to prove his contention by forcible arguments. First, he argues from the juristic principle: "*ubi lex non distinguit, nec nos distinguere debemus.*" The Code simply says "*ex Baptismo,*" without making any distinction between solemn

25. Cappello, "*De Sacramentis,*" III, 559.
26. St. Alphonsus, "*Theologia Moralis,*" lib·VI, 149.
27. Wernz, "*Jus Decretalium,*" IV, 489.
28. Vermeersch, "*Epitome Iuris Canonici,*" II, 51.
29. Vermeersch, "*Epitome Iuris Canonici,*" II, 340, ad 3.

Baptism and private regeneration. With one word, the legislator could have manifested his intention to restrict spiritual relationship to solemn Baptism; he failed to add that one word, therefore the presumption is that he did not intend to limit the extension of the term. In other words, the silence of the Code is positive, not negative: *"legislator, quod voluit, expressit; quod noluit, omisit."* The author of the Code knew that Baptism in the old law had been interpreted to mean private as well as solemn Baptism; he repeated the same word in the new law; there he intended the word Baptism in canon 768 to mean private no less than solemn Baptism.[30]

This argument assumes a brighter hue of probability when one reflects that in canon 762 an express exception is made of the sponsor in the supplying of ceremonies, but no such exception is proposed in regard to the godparent at the real, though private, Baptism. Cappello, however, seems to be guilty of a *petitio principii,* when he says that the opinion to which he now subscribes, was the only true one even in the old law.[31] For the group of eminent scholars who championed the contrary opinion, endowed it with the quality of probability, and the fact that even now Vermeersch apparently recognizes the formerly probable opinion, shows that the question is not definitely settled even under the present discipline, much less under the old legislation. At present, the practically unanimous opinion of canonists is that spiritual relationship arises from every valid Baptism, whether solemn or private.

Should the sponsor be represented at the ceremony by proxy, it is needless to say that the proxy contracts no spiritual relationship. This is manifest, because the proxy has neither been selected to be the sponsor by

30. Cappello, "*De Sacramentis,*" III, 560.
31. Cappello, "*De Sacramentis,*" III, 559.

the parents nor guardians, nor has he the intention of assuming this office personally—both of which are required for the validity of sponsorship.[32] The proxy is acting only by vicarious power, as agent for the sponsor actually designated. Accordingly the assumption of the office of sponsorship with all its concomitant obligations and rights, is made for the sponsor.

The minister of the sacrament also contracts a spiritual relationship with the person baptized. Since the impediment of spiritual relationship is of ecclesiastical origin, it can be contracted only by baptized persons. Hence, if the minister of Baptism was an infidel, there is no spiritual relationship, for such relationship presupposes Baptism as a condition *sine qua non.*[33] Furthermore, the infidel is in no way subject to purely ecclesiastical laws. This impediment, which consists of a mutual relation, can exist only when both parties are subject to the laws of the Church. Consequently, in the case of an infidel minister, there is no impediment on either party.[34]

The subsequent conversion of the infidel minister affects in no way his status in this regard. The relationship cannot revive because it never existed. Some held that the opposite opinion was not to be spurned.[35] However, it does not seem to rest on a solidly probable basis, because of the general principle: *"Non firmatur tractu temporis, quod de jure ab initio non subsistit."*[36]

The civil law is powerless to establish an impediment between an infidel minister and the person he baptizes. Such a law would be null and void for two reasons, viz., it is an invasion of the realm of the spiritual because it has to do with spiritual relationship, and the civil

32. canon 765, paragraphs 1 and 4.
33. Petrovits, "*The New Church Law on Matrimony,*" 386.
34. Cappello, "*De Sacramentis,*" III, 558.
35. Gasparri, "*De Matrimonio,*" 840.
36. Cappello, "*De Sacramentis,*" III, 558.

authority has no power to constitute matrimonial impediments where one of the parties is baptized.[37]

Prior to the Code, it was possible for the impediment of spiritual relationship to be multiplied many times. Each of two fathers, for instance, might sponsor the child of the other. In this case there arose a double compaternity. In the new law multiplication of the impediment is impossible, except in the extraordinary case where the minister acts also as sponsor by proxy.[38]

The Duties of Sponsors

The duties of godparents towards their spiritual charges are set forth in canon 769: *"Patrinorum est, ex suscepto munere, spiritualem filium perpetuo sibi commendatum habere, atque in iis quae ad christianae vitae institutionem spectant, curare diligenter ut ille talem in tota vita se praebeat, qualem futurum esse sollemni caeremonia spoponderunt."*

It is the solemn obligation of the sponsors to see to the moral and religious education of their godchildren through their whole life. Primarily, the natural parents of the child are obliged to care for the religious and moral upbringing of their offspring. The prescription of the ecclesiastical law requiring a sponsor is not an invasion of the parental right. It is true that the parents have the primary right to educate their child, and it is equally true that baptized children have the inalienable right to a Catholic education.[39] Consequently, if the parents are seriously negligent to their duty of giving their children a religious education, they forfeit their rights in this regard. It is but just, then, that children be assured of their spiritual education from another source. Accordingly the Church, in her solici-

37. Wernz, *"Jus Decretalium,"* IV, 490.
38. Noldin, *"De Sacramentis,"* 603.
39. canons 1113, 1335 and 1372.

tude, has placed this secondary obligation on the sponsors, the spiritual parents of the child. She has even gone into detail with regard to the duties of the sponsor in this connection. Thus, in canon 1335, it is specified that the sponsors are bound by the obligation *curandi ut omnes sibi subjecti vel commendati catechetica institutione erudiantur.*" Again, in canon 1372, is emphasized the obligations of the spiritual guardians to provide their charges with a Catholic education. The reason for these directions is obvious, for just as a well fed and well cared for child will normally grow up into a strong man or woman, so one that is trained in Christian duty, and nourished by Divine truth, will grow up into a well principled and well conducted Catholic.

If the child is to be reared in a Catholic family, the sponsors can presume that its moral education has been provided for.[40] There is, however, great danger that the child will not be rightly instructed if he is being reared among heretics. Here, if anywhere, the sponsor must vigilantly watch over the moral training of his spiritual child. It is only too true that the sponsor will be rendered helpless in many cases by the prejudices and bigotry of those in care of the child. In such a case, the sponsor need not be disquieted, for it is morally impossible for him to perform his duty. Since this duty revolves about a thing of the highest importance, the neglect of it is a mortal sin,[41] but the fact that this precept is one of purely ecclesiastical law makes it also true that a grave inconvenience excuses from the obligation.

40. St. Thomas, "*Summa Theologica*," III, q. 67, art. 8; Genicot-Salsmans, "*Institutiones Theologiae Moralis*," II, 157.

41. Genicot-Salsmans, "*Institutiones Theologiae Moralis*," II, 157.

BIBLIOGRAPHY

Sources

Acta Apostolicae Sedis, Rome, 1909-1924.

Acta Sanctae Sedis, Rome, 1865-1908.

Canones et Decreta Concilii Tridentini, Taurini, 1913.

Codex Iuris Canonici, Rome, 1918.

Codicis Iuris Canonici Fontes, Rome, 1923.

Collectanea S. Congregationis de Propaganda Fide, 2 vols., Rome, 1907.

Corpus Iuris Canonici, editio Lipsiensis II post Aemilii Ludovici Richteri curas ad librorum manu scriptorum et editionis Romanae fidem recognovit et ad notatione critica instruxit Aemilianus Friedberg, 2 vols., Lipsiae, 1922.

Corpus Iuris Civilis, Krueger-Mommsen, Berlin, 1895.

Rituale Romanum, Pauli V Pontificis Maximi jussu editum, et Benedicto XIV auctum et castigatum, Ratisbonae, 1901.

References

Alphonsus, Liguori, *Theologia Moralis*, Pariis, 1834.

Augustine, Rev. P. Charles, O. S. B., *A Commentary on the New Code of Canon Law*, 8 vols., St. Louis, 1920.

Bardenhewer, Otto, *Patrology* (*Shahan's Translation*), St. Louis, 1906.

Bingham, Joseph, *The Antiquities of the Christian Church*, London, 1878.

Binterim, Anton J., *Die Vorzueglichsten Denkwuerdigkeiten des Christ-Katholischen Kirche*, 16 Vols., Dusseldorf, 1816.

Blat, Albertus, O. P., *Commentarium Textus Codicis Iuris Canonici*, Romae, 1920.

Cappello, Felix M., S. J., *Tractatus Canonici-Moralis de Sacramentis juxta Codicem Iuris Canonici*, Taurini, 1920.

Chardon, Benedictini, P. D. C., *Dissertatio de Susceptoribus,* contained in *Disciplina Populi Dei,* a Claudio Fluery editio secunda, Venetiis, 1782.

Catechismus Concilii Tridentini, Taurini, 1914.

Catholic Encyclopedia, 16 Vols., New York, 1907-1912.

Catelanus, Joseph, *Rituale Romanum Benedicti Papae XIV,* Patavii, 1760.

Corblet, Jules, *Histoire du Sacrament de Bapteme,* 2 Vols., Geneva, 1882.

Coustant, Pierre, *Epistolae Romanorum Pontificum,* Parisiis, 1721.

De Smet, Aloysius, *De Sponsalibus et Matrimonio,* Brugis, 1923.

Devoti, Joannis, *Institutionum Canonicarum Libri IV,* Leodii, 1860.

Du Cange, *Glossarium ad Scriptores Mediae et Infimae Latinitatis,* Pariis, 1733.

Fagnanus, Prosperus, *Commentarium in Libros Decretalium,* Venetiis, 1696.

Feije, Henricus, *De Impedimentis et Dispensationibus,* Lovani, 1874.

Ferraris, F., Lucii, *Bibliotheca Canonica, Juridica, Moralis, Theologica, necnon Asetica, Polemica, Rubristica, Historica,* Parisiis, 1852.

Gasparri, Petrus, *Tractatus Canonicus de Matrimonio,* 2 Vols., Parisiis, 1904.

Genicot-Salsmans, *Institutiones Theologiae Moralis,* 2 Vols., Bruxellis, 1921.

Gury-Ballerini, *Compendium Theologiae Moralis,* Romae, 1874.

Harduin, *Acta Conciliorum,* 12 Vols., Parisiis, 1715.

Jundt, Isaac, *Dissertatio de Susceptoribus Baptismalium Origine,* Argentorati, 1755.

Kenrick, Francis P., *A Treatise on Baptism,* Baltimore, 1852.

Maroto, Philippus, *Institutiones Iuris Canonici,* Romae, 1919.

Martene, Edmund, O. S. B., *De Antiquis Ecclesiae Ritibus,* Rotomagi, 1700.

Mastrich, Gerald von, *Schediasma de Susceptoribus Infantium ex Baptismo, Eorumque Origine, Usu, et Abusu,* Duisbergo, 1670.

MPG—Migne, *Patrologia Graeca.*

MPL—Migne, *Patrologia Latina.*

Noval, Joseph, *De Processibus,* §I, *De Judiciis,* Romae, 1920.

Noldin, H., *De Sacramentis,* 3 Vols., Oeniponte, 1920.

Petrovits, Joseph, *The New Church Law on Matrimony,* Philadelphia, 1921.

Pesch, Christianus, *Praelectiones Dogmaticae,* 9 Vols., Freiburg, 1914.

Reiffenstuel, Anacletus, *Jus Canonicum Universum,* Venetiis, 1735.

Sanchez, Thoma, *De Sancto Matrimonii Sacramento Disputationum,* Venetiis, 1712.

Schmalzgrueber, Franciscus, *Jus Ecclesiasticum Universum,* Romae, 1845.

Schuler, Andraeus, *De Susceptoribus ex Historia Ecclesiastica,* Wittenberg, 1688.

Sohm, *Institutes of Roman Law* (Ledlie edition), Oxford, 1907.

SS. Concilia, *Sacrosancta Concilia, studio Philip. Labbei et Gabr. Cossarti,* 15 Vols., Parisiis, 1571.

Thomas Aquinas, *Summa Theologica,* Romae, 1894.

Trombelli, D. Joannis Chrysostomus, *Tractaus de Sacramentis,* 5 Vols., Bononiae, 1770.

Vecchiotti, Septimus, *Institutiones Canonicae,* Augustae Taurinorum, 1886.

Vlaming, Th. M., *Praelectiones Iuris Matrimonii,* 2 Vols., Bussum in Hollandia, 1923.

Vermeersch-Creusen, *Epitome Iuris Canonici, cum commentariis,* 3 Vols., Mechlinae-Romae, 1921.

Vicecomes, (Visconti), Joseph, *Observationes Ecclesiasticae de Antiquis Baptismi Ritibus ac Ceremoniis,* Parisiis, 1618.

Wernz, Franciscus Xav., S. J., *Jus Decretalium,* 6 tomes, Romae, 1908-1913.

Sacra Facultas Canonica

Universitas Catholica Americae

Washingtonii

1924-1925

No. 30

DEUS LUX MEA

THESES

QUAS

AD DOCTORATUS GRADUM

IN

IURE CANONICO

Apud Universitatem Catholicam Americae

CONSEQUENDUM

PUBLICE PROPUGNABIT

RICHARDUS JOSEPH KEARNEY

SACERDOS ARCHIDIOECESIS

PHILADELPHIENSIS

IURIS CANONICI LICENTIATUS

HORA III P. M. DIE XIX MAII A. D. MCMXXV

JUS CANONICUM

JUS PUBLICUM ECCLESIAE

ROMAN LAW

XLVIII. Tutela et Curatio
XLIX. Origin of Citizenship
L. Loss of Citizenship

International Law

LI. The Nature of International Law
LII. Sources and Principles of International Law
LIII. Treaties, Their Purpose and Scope
LIV. The General Rights and Obligations of States
LV. Diplomatic Agents
LVI. Consuls
LVII. Extradition
LVIII. The Monroe Doctrine
LIX. The Drago Doctrine
LX. The Right of Extra-territoriality

* * * * * *

Vidit Sacra Facultas:

PHILIPPUS BERNARDINI, S. T. D., J. U. D., Decanus.

H. LUDOVICUS MOTRY, S. T. D., J. C. D., a Secretis.

Vidit Rector Universitatis:

†THOMAS J. SHAHAN, S. T. D., J. U. L.

BIOGRAPHY

Richard Joseph Kearney was born on October 12, 1896, at Philadelphia, Pennsylvania. He received his primary education at the Hallowell Public School, and Saint Patrick's Parochial School. In September 1910, he entered the Roman Catholic High School, and four years later began his studies for the Priesthood at the Seminary of Saint Charles Borromeo, Overbrook, Pennsylvania. On May 26, 1923, he was ordained to the priesthood by His Eminence, D. Cardinal Dougherty.

On October 2, 1923, he entered the Catholic University of America at Washington, where he attended the lectures of Doctors Bernardini, Motry and Schaaf, on Canon Law; of Doctor Lima; on International Law, of Doctor Lardone on Roman Law.

To his professors he extends his grateful appreciation for their many kindnesses and services in his behalf.

www.ingramcontent.com/pod-product-compliance
Lightning Source LLC
LaVergne TN
LVHW050206080826
844660LV00012B/365

* 9 7 8 0 8 1 3 2 2 2 2 0 2 *